OTTERS IN THE HOUSE

OTTERS IN THE

HOUSE

By JOSEPH A. DAVIS

Illustrated with drawings by the author
and with photographs

Longman

LONGMAN GROUP LIMITED
London

*Associated companies, branches and
representatives throughout the world*

First published in Great Britain 1970

SBN 582 10805 5

Printed in Great Britain by
Lowe & Brydone (Printers) Ltd., London

To the memory of Mary C. W. Mitchell,
I dedicate this book she did not live to read.

Contents

Introduction

I suppose that if a man is going to share his home with an otter, or worse, two of them, it's really nobody's business but his own, just as it is if he wants to walk around with a pimento stuck in his ear. Unless he's a great deal more aloof from the world than I am, though, he will feel constrained at some point to offer some explanation.

I had got myself involved with otters intentionally, deliberately, and with as full knowledge of the consequences as anyone could have before the fact. I was Curator of Mammals at the Bronx Zoo and thus, by definition, an expert in the field of coping with wild animals of every description. Part of my job demanded that I have an understanding of the basics, at least, of animal behavior, and this meshed very neatly with a lifelong interest in the subject.

Up to my early twenties, observing what animals did was just a pastime; my sprouting professional interests were focused on systematics—the study of the evolutionary relationships of species—and as far as I knew at the time such study was restricted to the cleaned and preserved remains of specimens killed for the purpose. Then, in my first year of graduate school at Cornell, I attended a series of special lectures by the visiting ethologist, Konrad Lorenz. Until that time I had not read his book, *King Solomon's Ring,* and in fact (I'm ashamed to admit) had never heard of his field, which proved to be the scientific study of the behavior of animals. Even a lesser man could not have kept from dazzling me with the realization that animal-watching could be useful as well as entertaining, but this was Konrad Lorenz himself. This was Konrad Lorenz, who illustrated a point on the blackboard with a vast Thurber-like drawing, who could mime the courtship ritual of a duck without losing a snip of his dignity. Suddenly there opened up a vast new world that would supplement the measurement of skulls in a museum.

The distinction between ethology and its elder sister science, animal psychology, was once put rather strongly by a convert from psychology to ethology in these terms: the ethologist *studies* animals, while the psychologist *uses* them. The aims of the two fields are different, and each has its merits. Behavior is the prime interest of the psychologists (at least of those I've known), and they are interested in animals only as the vessels in which behavior is expressed. Their eye seems always to be on human behavior, and some study *the* rat, *the* cat, and *the* monkey only as a means to understanding man, with little concern for the vast spectrum of animal life. This approach is legitimate as long as the psychologist remembers that *the* rat is only one kind out of a vast array of species of rats, and as long as his prime concern is behavior itself and he doesn't try to generalize then about the behavior of rats in general. The ethologist on the other hand is first and foremost

a zoologist. His interest lies in the animal, and then in its behavior, because that behavior is a part of the totality of the
animal. He may hope to understand human behavior (doesn't
everyone?), but generally this is secondary to his interest in the
animal as an animal. The psychologist may seek to discover
whether a domestic cat can distinguish between two sounds that
vary slightly in pitch, as a means to understanding sound discrimination in man, or sound discrimination per se. The
ethologist on the other hand may be interested in the same
phenomenon, but he is more likely to want to know because
he's investigating the significance of vocalizations in the social
life of the cat. So ethology, then, is the business of seeing what
an animal does, and trying to discover the significance of its
behavior in terms of the animal's biological makeup. It has
been my excuse for keeping animals at home with me, or one of
my excuses anyway.

Now that I've given my reason for being interested in
studying the behavior of animals and indicated that I'm interested particularly in otters, a question may arise. If I'm so keen
on discovering what otters do, and why they do it, why didn't
I go out and study them in their wild haunts instead of bringing them into a suburban cottage? The answer is fairly simple;
better zoologists than I, with far more field experience, have
never seen a wild otter. Apart from the fact that my fellow man
and I have pretty much succeeded in driving the North American otter out of this area by covering the landscape with houses
and people, and by fouling the watercourses with our waste,
almost any handbook on mammals will say that the otters of
this and other continents are nocturnal and shy. Otters *are* shy,
which is to say they're too intelligent to show themselves to
their greatest enemy. And they *are* largely nocturnal, but for the
same reason. Otters can and do hunt at night occasionally in
places where man does not disturb them, but the otter has not

lived that would be strictly nocturnal, given a choice. So I could go out in the field, and if I were lucky could get a glimpse of an otter now and then—but from a distance that would hinder observation,* and I would have to guess at the significance of much that I saw. Living with tame otters provides a biased picture of their behavior, but because of the give and take involved it gives insights that are unavailable to the man who only watches. My experiences with otters in my home will make it easier some day for some observer in the field, in the otter's home, to understand what he sees. I confess, too, that I hope the observer turns out to be me.

* One vocalization, the "chuckle," is not audible from more than five or six yards away; it happens to be one of the crucial sounds to be noted in a comparative study of otter species.

OTTERS IN THE HOUSE

1 Things That Go Bump in the Night

Mary and I had not really intended to get into the bathtub together; it was one of those things forced upon us by grim necessity. Samaki, that stinking otter—literally stinking, because in the weeks since his arrival he had abjured virtually all external contact with water—Samaki peered at us as apprehensively as a demon cornered in a baptistry. It had become evident to all three of us that the time had come when Sam's introduction to water could no longer be put off.

A few minutes before, I had drawn a tubful of water and slid shut the shower doors, leaving them unlocked. Naturally enough, Sam worked at one door with his nose and soon had it open. Then he lolled at the rim of the tub and peered in, with no intention of further action. I turned my back for a moment and Mary seized her chance. She scooped up the otter and dumped him into the water with a resounding splash that told me what had happened. It took me only the barest fraction of a second to spin around, but by that time Sam stood dripping on the floor, permeated as much with chagrin as with water. Otters have terribly quick reflexes.

It was nearly a month since I had relieved Mary of her burden of quarantining the half-grown spot-necked otter. She had made the hour's drive from her Westchester home to mine in New Jersey with the avowed purpose of putting an end to "all this nonsense about the tub." The truth was that she missed Sam. Had he already learned to swim in the tub she would have come over to see *that*.

Mary Mitchell was old enough to be my mother, as she often reminded me, usually as the preamble to a lecture vainly intended to reform one or another of my foibles. She had some years earlier appointed herself my principal unsolicited adviser in areas that ranged from my supervision of the Bronx Zoo's Department of Mammals to my dietary habits. About the time I met Mary a children's book on mammals that I had written was published, and on the flap the publisher described me as "a world authority" on the subject. Mary had never let me hear the end of it; any second now I expected to hear her utter those well-worn words, "Well, *you're* The World Authority—let's see *you* do it, Buster." I moved adroitly to forestall her.

"Damn it all, Mary," I said, "you ought to know that you don't just heave an otter into a tub to teach him to swim. You have to do these things" (I paused for effect) "intelligently." That got her. I noted a slight arching of an eyebrow; score one for me.

With what I hoped was a cool professional air, I drained the tub and stepped into it. Mary followed skeptically, while Samaki dallied in the bathroom doorway. I closed the shower doors and we stood there, cramped and feeling not a little ridiculous. As the seconds plodded by, The World Authority began to search frantically for a face-saving phrase with which to terminate the abortive demonstration—then, as I was still grop-ing for a graceful exit line, the insatiable curiosity I had been counting on did its work on Sam. The door slid open and the otter poked his head through. He entered, but only to stay momentarily on the narrow ledge at that end of the tub, and he exited quickly lest some new aqueous disaster befall him. He repeated his in-and-out performance several times but he stead-fastly refused to slide down into the tub itself, and that was as far as we could go for the day. But at least I had succeeded in luring him into the tub *enclosure*. From here on in things would have to be done slowly and patiently. And preferably without an audience.

Later that afternoon, after Mary had left, I found myself thinking back on the day's events, particularly the absurd con-clave in the tub when, at the expense of my tarnished dignity, I had so barely made good on my rash boast that I knew how to outthink a mere otter. At such times it is all too easy to yield to the insidious temptations of common sense and to wonder how any such outlandish and improbable situation could have been allowed (much less *made*) to come to pass within the sanctity of my home. And because both my spirit and my flesh tend to soften into mush in times of self-dissection, I began to wonder anew just how it was that I found myself sharing less than a thousand square feet of suburban floor space divided between two otters, one seemingly afraid of water and the other adamantly resentful of her eager would-be companion.

I suppose the whole thing can be said to have begun when I decided to buy a house of my own. When I went to work at the Zoo I was still living with my parents in that bastion of grime and civic decay, Jersey City, but I realized that I would inevitably have to move, and began the search. No matter how tolerant, or at times even enthusiastic, my parents were about sharing their living space with wild animals, it had always been obvious to me that I *was* imposing on them when I brought home another animal. Holes chewed by a kangaroo in a prominent location in two hundred square feet of carpeting are, after all, laughable only in the other family's house, and I can't say that I looked forward to seeing the newly installed carpet going the way of the old. Moreover, I looked anxiously toward the day when I could quit my depressing hometown.

While the house-hunt went on, so did a search for an animal. Two species have for years been as fascinating to me as they were unattainable. Otters have had a place in my affection for about half of my life, ever since, as a kid, I read of Emil Liers and his experiences with them. In the fall of 1959, before the suburban house was more than an unjelled wish, I found and bought a barely weaned otter cub of a South American species from a pet shop I had visited in search of a monkey for the Zoo. He came home with me crusted in his own diarrhea, suffering from incipient rickets, and with one milky eye. At his age he feared water that was deep enough to make him lose firm contact with the bottom of the tub, but because of his diarrhea we had to bathe him frequently. This we did, in tepid water, only as often as necessity demanded, toweled him as thoroughly as we could—which left him far from dry—and put him to sleep under a heat lamp. I knew virtually nothing about otters in a practical sense at that time, and assumed that very young cubs lacked the water-resistant quality of pelage that the adults had. To a degree this is true, but although I have not yet seen a healthy otter cub of comparable age (they all enter this country in less than prime condition) I have a hunch that by weaning age they are normally waterproof. A healthy otter emerges from the water with only the long, glossy guard hairs wet, and these tend to clump together to give the animal a rough appearance. The otter's dense, woolly underfur resists wetting and insulates the body from both cold air and water by trapping warm air among the fibers. Given a chance, a wet otter rubs itself on absorbent material—earth, leaves, moss—or simply air-dries, after a brief, doglike shake. A tame otter can be dried rapidly by a quick rub-down with a towel if it is healthy, while a sick one never seems to dry properly. The water-shedding quality of the under-fur is apparently produced by an oily secretion of the skin, and when an otter "loses condition" this oil production seems to be one of the first body functions to be curtailed.

The otter cub never recovered from his weakened state and despite our precautions succumbed within a fortnight. But during the time we had him he managed to captivate everyone who came in contact with him. For Ottie the world ended a foot or two above ground, and to him I seemed to be only a pair of feet to be adored at all times, followed earnestly when in motion, and draped across when at rest. Young cubs I've seen since then also displayed this myopic behavior, and apparently the condition is normal at that age. Still, Ottie was no acrophobe, and when picked up he would content himself in hanging as limp as a ferret, in any position, totally unconcerned. He died a lifelong friend of two weeks.

Months later, after I found my house and after I had succeeded in putting otters, and particularly Ottie, out of my mind, Gavin Maxwell's *Ring of Bright Water* was published. It rekindled my longing for an otter but, I reasoned, a mortgage and an otter add up to more than a curator has at hand, and I looked for another species, little realizing how soon another otter would come along.

The other species had captivated me eight years before, at the

Bronx Zoo. Having received permission to enter the Zoo two hours before it opened to the public so that I could take photos of a kinkajou-like marsupial called a cuscus, I passed by the series of enclosures known as the Burrowing Rodent Cages. There were no rodents in evidence, but in one cage a pair of enormous ears met my glance. Under them trotted a small tawny fox several sizes too small for such appendages. It was a fennec, a small desert-dweller from North Africa. It trotted from side to side along the concrete coping of the enclosure,

whining a peculiarly appealing little *weee-weee-weee* sound, and when I leaned forward over the guard wire the fox flopped to the ground and rolled onto its side, *weee*-ing and presenting to me its fluffy back. The animal looked for all the world as if it were asking to be petted, but I was cautious—doubly so. For one thing, as a visitor to the Zoo I had no business crossing the guard wire. I hesitated. Then, furtively, I stepped over the wire. No one came shouting after me, for the keeper was indoors attending to other charges. Next I inserted a pencil through the wire-mesh cage front and tentatively stroked the submissive canine sprite. It wiggled a little but stayed for more, so I replaced the pencil with my finger.

house they seemed far too loud for such a small animal: he would jump down from a cabinet or from the chair that was his "den" with a heavy-footed thump or leap upon a throw-rug and skid across the floor deafeningly. The floor adjacent to two hot-air registers instilled him with an atavistic urge to dig; his

scrabbling went on sporadically through the nights, getting him nowhere, but apparently satisfying a compulsion. His hard-rubber ball, ignored all evening, thumped and rumbled solidly in seemingly constant motion some nights, and on others alternated with a thick hollow one that had a bell inside.

Occasionally a new sound would ring out and usually brought me groping forth to investigate and swear oaths of destruction upon my spirited tenant. There were times, however, when sleep seemed more urgent, and although I should have known better I stayed put. On the morning after one such unfamiliar thump I awoke to a spectacle of the type that just isn't suitable for pre-breakfast consumption. I greet each dawn with a minimum of fortitude to begin with, and until I get my vital processes in gear even a sock with a hole in the toe is liable to cast doubt on the advisibility of leaving the bedroom at all. I had already left the bedroom though, and was standing in the doorway of the former master bedroom which now held my desk and books. This room, with its louvered double doors, was, with the small bedroom and bath, off limits to Pixie, and relatively clean. The living room and kitchen before me were horrible to behold. Black footprints were everywhere, focused upon an unstoppered bottle of India ink lying on its side.

But some good may come of even the worst disaster. First I stood there numbly. Then I hurled the threats and imprecations expected of me. And then I set about to see what I could find in the situation that would keep Pixie from having scored all of the points in the round. Oddly enough, there *was* something of value. At least I had a beautiful record of the fox's nocturnal wanderings.

Fennec footprints are not very doglike despite the basic similarity of the feet. The hair that grows between the pads is long in a fennec, and obscures the imprint of the pads. Even worse, in this situation anyway, the hairs soaked up ink like brushes, dispensing it for a long time and over great distance. With difficulty I could tell the front end of the prints and determine Pixie's direction, and thus the sequence of part of his activities.

Pixie had some time before learned how to get onto the dining-room table by jumping first to the window sill next to it. I had met this fact head-on by keeping the tabletop clear of small objects, particularly ink bottles. Human memory is fallible, alas, and that was why the ink bottle now reposed on the floor.

Pixie had jumped to the table and knocked the bottle over, dislodging its stopper just enough to spill ink. He had then descended to the floor via the window sill after pushing the bottle and stopper off the table. Following this the fox trotted about the rooms, visiting the kitchen and the space under the sofa, and then he jumped up on his favorite chair. From there the tracks seemed to fade and be replenished accidentally when he passed through the pool of ink. Fortunately the novelty of the ink seemed not to hold his interest.

Over the next few days I managed to scour off most of the tracks, but I left the ones on the window sill, and in the past seven years they have served as an insistent reminder to me. I haven't repeated my mistake. I've made new ones, but never again that one.

Our first autumn brought a new detail to be coped with. One of the things I liked about the house was its fireplace. Through the first winter and summer other considerations occupied me, but with the advent of cool weather again I began to look forward to the comforts of a fire. Pixie had been making regular forays through the hanging mesh fire screen all along, and I had paid this little heed since (as I realized later) the fireplace was empty and clean. After the first fire, things changed. Bits of charcoal began to turn up on the floor, and sooty smudges on the sofa cushion. Several attempts at circumventing Pix's visits failed and I was faced with the choice of having either a fennec or a fireplace; I could not have both. I boarded up the fireplace. Well, not really boarded it—I erected a removable barricade made of a piece of hardboard held in place with two cement blocks, but maneuvering the apparatus proved so cumbersome that it became almost permanent. Recently it was replaced by an expensive frame with heat-tempered glass doors.

Housebreaking the fennec was for a long time no more than a minor problem. Pixie took naturally, if not invariably, to a little pan filled with dry clay particles. His habit of entering and leaving the pan at full speed scattered clay over the floor, and the loud crunching underfoot when I walked got on my nerves. Setting the pan inside a low cardboard box that Pix had to jump over solved that annoyance nicely. One other matter caused concern for a while. Pixie, in true fox-fashion, cached uneaten food for future consumption. Much of his caching he did in the same litter pan, but fennecs apparently have indestructible innards and when he didn't become ill I stopped worrying. The caches I never could grow to accept, though, were those that turned up behind the sofa cushions, each one accompanied by a less than beatific halo of grease possessed of a stubborn immortality that had been denied its now-gamy source.

Up to now Pixie has been emerging as an unadulterated nuisance, and the picture is not entirely true. He did have one redeeming quality, perhaps more important than it may seem. Pixie preyed upon ants. Strangely, for a house in a fairly undeveloped area, our home had been remarkably free of household pests (other than fennecs). Any mouse hapless enough to enter would, I am certain, fall victim to Pix, but of mice we saw none. I have on occasion found foraging carpenter ants—those large black ones that nest in wood. Several times Pixie reached them before I did and with lips drawn back he would pounce upon the ant, mincing it with his incisors. Foxes and many other carnivores are known to dine upon insects, so Pixie's behavior was not unexpected. During his tenancy, I must say, ants rarely lived long enough in the house for me to see them.

Although fennecs are nocturnal creatures, they may often be

seen basking in the sunlight, at least in captivity. His favorite sunbathing place was a cabinet set under the large casement window on the west wall of the living room, and after Pix had been with me a short time my next-door neighbor remarked on the "chihuahua" he had seen sitting at the window. Fortunately, at close range Pixie's vulpine nature was unmistakable, and I had no trouble with the policeman who rang the bell one day to ask if I had an unlicensed dog in the house.

Pixie never really lost his wildness and distrust of humans. With a great deal of patience I could, for a time, lure him close enough to accept bits of food from my hand. When I placed myself so that he could stand on a rug to accept the food he was more self-assured, but this was because the rug provided better traction for a quick getaway. Nimble as he was, the linoleum tile floor, even unwaxed, turned any sudden start into a display reminiscent of the old movie cartoons, where a character's feet spun ineffectually for a long, perilous moment before he began to move. This characteristic of the floor was later to cause Pix to lose many a dash away from a relatively slow, flat-footed otter.

2 Like a Soft and Loose-Skinned Puppy

My formal commitment to otters began with a letter from Dora Weyer. Living with her husband on a rubber plantation in Liberia, Dora passed her time rearing young animals she bought from the natives and selling them, after they were weaned, to zoos.

One New Year's Day an otter cub had been seen swimming weakly down a nearby river. Too young by far to be on his own, it seemed likely, as Dora said, that his mother had met with an untimely end—doubtless at human hands—and that he had been driven by starvation to crawl from the den in search of her. How long he had been in the river no one knew. Late that night he was brought to Dora's home, sold to her, and thus given his first tenuous chance for survival.

Dora's first night with the cub gave little hope; he was emaciated and feeble, and refused all forms of nourishment. But Joey, as Dora christened him later, was tenacious of life and he managed to learn to accept a human-type baby bottle, even though its nipple was abnormally large for him. A second problem that Dora's acuteness conquered quickly was that of the milk formula. To my knowledge the composition of otter milk has never been determined. Milk is nòt a simple substance by any means; the amount of butterfat and sugar, to name but two constituents, varies from one species of mammal to another, as does the proportion of total solids to water. Most carnivore babies (dogs, cats, ferrets, civets, etc.) are sufficiently tolerant of "wrong" formulas to grow on evaporated cow's milk properly diluted. Too weak a dilution, though, and the cub is undernourished; too rich a formula and it develops diarrhea, and subsequent problems.

The first attempts to induce the otter cub to accept evaporated milk in a dilution normal for rearing young carnivores met with obstinate refusal. Under such circumstances a good Animal Person abandons the "reasonable" approach and tries something less orthodox. Dora *was* a good Animal Person, and because she was, she soon hit upon a formula that Joey would accept without subsequent upset and it rapidly restored the cub's health. She wrote, almost apologetically, that Joey's taste ran to straight, undiluted evaporated milk, with a raw egg yolk added to each four ounces. Normally such a rich formula ought to have a catastrophic outcome but, as Dora wrote, the great quantities of water Joey drank after each feeding seemed to dilute it properly inside him, because no enteric problems arose. The cub learned to lie on his back, holding the bottle in his little hands,* but like all otter cubs he could not be trusted

---

* It is almost too precise to refer to the "paws" of otters, for even in the more typical species they serve as more than mere locomotory apparatus. Most of the otters, including all those of the genus *Lutra*, have feet differentiated into two forms: the broad hind feet, which are essentially limited to the functions of feet; and the forefeet, which, in addition to acting as support for

with his milk in a bowl. To an otter, any liquid in a bowl invites bathing, and evaporated milk, even without raw egg, isn't very good for otter fur—or for those parts of the household the otter then comes into contact with.

Two days after his arrival at the Weyers' Joey was guzzling fourteen ounces in four feedings, with between-meal snacks of cooked chicken and all the water he wanted. His vitality increased markedly, and as it did Dora found him dogging her heels constantly, eager for any and all attention, whether it was being rolled over and over on the floor or simply being held. In Dora's words the little otter was in almost every respect "just like a very soft and loose-skinned puppy." But of course he was an otter, and one that had already learned to swim, so that water of any kind drew him irresistibly. Before long the Weyers' bathtub became the focus of Joey's daily activity, and the principal source of respite for Dora from the insistent affection of the cub. At such times he was content to be alone with his water, as he was content to fall into solitary sleep after each feeding. The desire to sleep, by the way, came on precipitously, and when it did Joey would simply cease the activity of the moment, waddle off to his bed, and collapse. No force on earth could deter him when he felt like a nap.

I decided without too much soul-searching that I would ask Dora to sell the otter to me, and she agreed. Had the Zoo not been replete with otters I might have had a hard time deciding who should get him, as I had the year before when I bought another otter for the Zoo over my urge to buy her myself. She became the victim of a then unforeseeable accident. At that time I had read Maxwell's account of the near-death that one

---

quadrupedal movement, are often used to manipulate objects and hence may in truth be called "hands." I find this distinction between hands and feet useful in describing many of the otters' actions, and will use it frequently in the remainder of the book.

of his otters underwent through overheating caused by its excitement at being enclosed in a crate, but somehow I had never mentioned it to Dora, who had not yet been able to get the book. The Weyers constructed a crate for the otter that would have been perfect for any other kind of animal, and well enough ventilated despite their having limited the vent ports in size. These they made very small (wire mesh is almost impossible to obtain where they live) because they feared that the otter's penchant for reaching out might cause her hand to be crushed if a neighboring crate shifted in loading or on the flight. The result was that the otter arrived dead. Compounding the tragedy, Dora and her teen-aged daughter Dianne were on the same plane, and were subjected to the heartbreaking sight of the magnificent animal, rigid in death.

Dora had her first otter's death still very much in her mind as she and her husband made preparations for Joey's flight. Early in January she wrote that she had prevailed upon a Mr. Grace, of Pan American, to let Joey ride in the pilot's cockpit with him, so that he could keep an eye on the cub and help if Joey showed signs of distress. Airline rules required that the crate be no more than a given size—eighteen inches in the longest dimension.

Complications then set in with suddenness and persistence. Mr. Grace had to postpone his trip indefinitely, and while Dora searched for another chaperon Joey grew in size and vigor.

The second complication came from the otter himself; in spite of the indomitable spirit that had brought him through that perilous New Year's Day, Joey had become vulnerable to fear. Dora wrote of an incident of a seemingly trivial nature which augured ill for the transatlantic journey to come.

Joey had been sleeping at night closed in a large wicker basket in a room that also housed at large two young genets, catlike members of the civet family. Like most young carnivores the genets were full of devilment (as the otter was), but after teasing him they could, and did, escape to sanctuary on high objects in the room. The otter by now was strong enough to defend himself, and to turn the tables on them, for that matter. And that was what worried Dora—that if Joey escaped from his basket and pursued his arboreal roommates he might somehow climb high enough above the floor to fall and injure himself. So Dora contrived a simple solution to the problem—she moved his basket into the living room, next to the buffet under which Joey preferred to nap by day. Very sensibly she did this in the morning, to give the cub a full day in which to grow accustomed to the basket's new location.

At bedtime Dora followed her usual routine scrupulously. She deposited the cub in his basket with his regular sleeping towel and a supply of chicken to busy him during the first critical moments. Then she closed and covered the basket and retreated to her own room. Anxious minutes passed as the Weyers listened in silence for the sharp, whistle-like chirp that the cub used as a summons, but it didn't come, and they went to bed. Hardly had they begun to relax, however, when the sound of a violent struggle reached Dora's ears; Joey was tearing at the basket. In the uncertain moments while she debated whether or not to go to the frightened cub a second sound burst forth, a sound that caused her to think he was choking on a wicker fragment and sent her rushing into the living room. As Dora hurried to him, calling to him, she was answered by a hideous, heart-rending howl, and when she took him into her arms the cub clung to her with all his strength. His body was hot, the naked skin of his little paws febrile, and his breath came in great racking gasps—the "choking" sounds Dora had heard. This was the aftermath of panic and all because the little otter was alone in a "new" place. A long spell in a water-filled tub restored Joey's temperature to normal and he quickly forgot his experience. But for Dora, and later for me, the incident boded no good.

At Dora's request I checked with the Zoo's veterinarian on the matter of a tranquilizer for the cub, who now weighed eight pounds. I sent suggestions on crate design, for Dora had come to see that a wicker basket would not contain Joey. She was concerned that a too-well-ventilated container, even in the pilot's compartment, might subject the little otter to serious chill. For warmth the crate would be generously supplied with rags, and Joey's habit of covering any nocturnal droppings with part of his towel should serve to keep the bedding reasonably clean.

Dora went on in a subsequent letter to describe the long experiments she carried on with a tranquilizer, beginning with a small dose and working up to one that kept Joey soothed for the equivalent in time of the flight from Liberia to New York. She told me that she had prevailed upon friends, the De-Coudres, to baby-sit Joey in transit. For reasons that will unfold later I did not have the pleasure of meeting Joey's guardian angels, but my gratitude to them when I saw the otter alive and well at the airport was augmented later by Dora's account, in another letter, of the events that preceded the flight, and what happened en route.

On the evening of the flight Joey took his injection of tranquilizer and allowed himself to be placed in the crate, to which he had become accustomed over the previous few days. He was quiet, probably dozing, until the Weyers took the crate into their car, at which point he began to tear vainly at the box. Dora's attempt to soothe him by speaking softly triggered howls of anguish; her husband Al turned the car around and they returned home, where they gave Joey a second dose of the drug.

Under the influence of this double dose the little otter had subsided into sleep by the time he was turned over to the De-Coudres in the waiting room at the Robertsfield Airport. Joey remained asleep until the deafening roar of the plane coming into the small field brought him out of his torpor. Instantly he was frantic—he began to claw his way under the rag bedding, and just as Mrs. DeCoudres was sure that he would suffocate the rags parted enough for the broad pink nose to show. The little handlike paws were pressed over his ears.

Mrs. DeCoudres carried Joey's crate aboard without further incident, but on the long trip she was to be a very hardworking guardian. Every time Joey showed signs of having regained consciousness she opened the top enough to pass in some of the cooked chicken Dora had supplied. By the time the jet set down at New York, Joey had consumed all of the chicken—Dora had packed enough to last through any delay en route—an egg, and a generous portion of Mr. DeCoudres' breakfast steak. The effects of the tranquilizer, augmented by the cub's greedy preoccupation with food and his tendency to sleep off a meal, had saved him from a return of panic.

When I knew that Joey would soon arrive I located a cub at a dealer's in New York. Recalling Maxwell's contention that his otters could stand only limited solitude, I had begun to think that Joey might need a companion for the hours I was away each day. This cub, of a South American species, was a tiny thing, its eyes only just opened, and it was too young to have made the long air journey unattended. The cub, a female, I named Flump. Because she was far too young to leave at home, I had to bring her to work each day and feed her at intervals. She was still only at the crawling stage, so a low cardboard box in the office held her, but the winter weather combined with the inefficiency of the Volkswagen's heater meant that I had to reinstate the procedure I had used with a baby wallaby I had reared a few years before—the cub rode under my sweater in the car. Recently I had taken to wearing a vest, but it soon became obvious that, despite Flump's being wrapped first in one of the wallaby's old pouches, prudence demanded that I wear my oldest, most frayed shirts and sweaters. Her metabolic wastes were inclined to be liquid.

Before I knew it, Joey's day of arrival was upon us. I awoke on the morning of 9 February at four-thirty, looked at my wrist watch and realized that I had a half hour's sleep yet to go. The day before I had told my telephone wake-up service to ring me at five instead of the usual seven o'clock, so my remaining slumber was peaceful. It was absolutely serene, right up to six-thirty, when I awakened again. Could I have slept through, despite the ringing phone? There wasn't time for speculation, and somehow I managed to do in twenty minutes what I had planned to do in an hour or more. First a phone call to Pan American to confirm the plane's arrival (hoping it would be late), but the plane had made good time and would be in fifteen minutes early, at six forty-five. Washing and dressing accomplished themselves somewhat haphazardly, and somewhere in that time I fed Flump. While I put Joey's milk formula on the stove to warm it I downed a quick Coke, in large gulps that were later to result in a spectacular belch. Warmed, the formula went into a thermos bottle, which I packed into a paper bag along with six hard-boiled eggs and two foil packets of broiled and boiled chicken (Dora had said only "cooked" chicken, so I was taking no chances). At a few minutes to seven I dashed to the car with everything, including the cub snuggled against my belly, pumped the accelerator, and turned the ignition switch. The starter chugged briskly but the motor wouldn't turn over. I tried again. And again. Nothing. Maybe I had flooded the motor. I waited, not very calmly, with visions of a frantic, panting otter near death.

Better call the airport and leave word for the DeCoudres, at the same time letting the extra gas work out of the motor. As I reached the phone it rang, and the pleasant maternal voice that so often woke me of late was telling me that it was seven-fifteen, and she'd been ringing since seven. Somehow I kept my voice at a normal level and asked why she had not called me at five o'clock. She had not been so instructed, she answered, with a hint of sorrow in her tone; obviously the message had never reached her. I barked something about a plane from Africa and a dying otter, I think, and hung up. Then I called Pan Am to get word to the DeCoudres that I would arrive somehow, but not soon.

Back at my usually dependable Volkswagen things were no better. During my next attempt to start the motor I caught myself threatening the car through clenched teeth; I drew a deep breath and exhaled slowly. The tension didn't decrease a whit, but from that point on my mental processes became a little more orderly. The driveway looked somewhat more level than it was, so that I was unable to push the car. With reverse gear engaged, the starting motor brought it tantalizingly near the street, and then the battery died. At last a passing truck driver helped me gain the street, but coasting down the hill did no more than get me to the bottom, from which point I trotted to the service station, hoping that Flump would tolerate her kangaroo-style ride. She did.

There is an inexorable rule of nature that if anything can go wrong in an already bad situation, it will go wrong, and often does so, in multiples.

So it was that when I reached the station I learned the tow-truck was unavailable for the moment. At that point I made three phone calls: to a Zoo colleague who lived nearby, Dorothy Reville, asking if I might borrow her old Ford; to Pan Am asking that the DeCoudres leave the otter at the airport A.S.P.C.A. shelter if they had to leave before I arrived; and to a taxi office for transportation to the Revilles'. When I got there, Dorothy was dressed and offered to drive me out to Idlewild Airport in their new Falcon. It was eight o'clock.

The drive to Idlewild was uneventful. We took the long way around, past the Zoo, because neither of us was familiar with the direct route, and we had little desire to chance getting lost in the height of the morning rush-hour. I had Flump sleeping in her sack under my jacket, but I felt a little uneasy about wearing my green vest rather than the old sweater I had taken to wearing since Flump's arrival. As it turned out, my vest and shirt were safe, but on the evening ride home the little otter slipped out of her sack and so unobtrusively plastered the front of my trousers with chartreuse excrement that I never knew it until I had been home nearly an hour.

At the Pan Am counter I inquired about my otter, and one of the men said something about throwing cold water on it. My heart sank, but he assured me that it was alive and at the A.S.P.C.A. shelter. After a small contretemps trying to find the place where Dorothy was parked (she was just locking the car as I ran up clutching my Flump-bloated abdomen), we found the shelter and in it a turquoise crate containing a groggy little otter. At my approach he vented an explosive snort of alarm and warning. Slowing my movements and speaking softly, I examined the animal, saw that he was in no real distress, and covered the crate with a cloth Dora had sent along. Joey was quiet on the trip to the Zoo, and throughout the day. We opened his crate inside a cage in the animal hospital, but he never ventured out. He accepted a hard-boiled egg from me, and a little chicken, but he remained groggy. Despite this, he snorted at a keeper who set down a dustpan under the wire floor of the cage.

At the opposite end of the room were our three young orangs. They had been an expensive purchase, but were necessary if we were ever to have breeding orangs, for our adult pair had shown no inclination to mate properly. We were lucky to get these youngsters, but unlucky to have got in the bargain a seemingly inexhaustible supply of internal parasites. We had treated them for those parasites that had been found upon examination, but no sooner would the veterinarian kill off one kind than a different one would pop up. Or the orangs would come down with the sniffles, and by now they had been in the hospital for months, what with their initial quarantine and their subsequent difficulties. We pampered them and guarded their health jealously. Today they began banging their food pans as I watched Joey. Although he paid no heed to the noise, I was so concerned lest the tranquilizer wear off and he become upset that I could almost have strangled the three apes.

Somehow we were spared about an hour of the long day ahead for us. For the rest of the morning and into the afternoon I worked half-heartedly on routine stuff, and managed to avoid descents of small groups of architectural students assigned to design zoo buildings (they would come back next week together). Carl Berger, the illustrator, dropped in for some technical assistance in the matter of dog evolution, providing a welcome diversion, and the only one that took my mind off Joey for a while. Then it began to snow, and by four o'clock Dorothy and I decided to leave for home before the two inches of snow grew any deeper. We bundled Joey's crate in the car, and with Flump stirring restlessly under my coat, set out for New Jersey. Our progress was slow under the unpredictable road conditions, and we passed the scenes of perhaps half a dozen accidents in the twenty-seven-mile trip home.

We picked up Bob Reville and deposited our otters at my house; then the Revilles took me shopping for otter food, and to pick up my car which had apparently suffered nothing more than a clogged fuel line. Dorothy helped me to stock up on chicken, and eventually we returned to look in on Joey, who was more alert but seemingly glued into his crate.

Later, when Joey and I were alone, I began to tempt, or try to tempt, him from what I had expected him to think of as a prison, but which now he obviously regarded as the only famil-iar sanctuary in a foreign place. He took a hard-boiled egg from me, but his manner was desultory. He refused any chicken. He reached out for his bottle, but pulled it into the crate and seemed more interested in tearing the nipple out than in get-ting milk. I ran the shower, then filled the tub, and while Joey perked up and emerged as far as his shoulders, he stayed in his box amidst the now soaked and fouled bedding. He wanted water, but not enough to come out for it. Finally I held the water pan for him within his reach and he drank greedily, then sloshed his doll's hands into it. I bounced balls for him, made a ramp of plywood, and tried all my enticements again, but clearly he wasn't ready to step over the threshold of his crate from Africa into the New World. At eight-thirty he fell asleep, hand in his mouth, sucking away quietly. I left him and finished a letter to Dora, reassuring her that her otter was well.

Joey awoke at ten-forty-five and ate several of the chicken hearts that by now formed the bulk of Pixie's diet. On my way to bed a few minutes past one o'clock, I decided to try just once more. I don't remember what it was that did the trick—I think it was a rolling rubber ball—but suddenly Joey was teetering on the edge of the crate and then he was out on the floor.

3   An Abrasive Affection

Eight pounds of otter cub regarded me warily, understandably enough, since he had been aware of me thus far only in conjunction with a series of totally strange sounds, scents, and sights. But young animals, and particularly young otters, generally seem to trust humans, unless they have by experience learned the contrary. Almost before I knew what was happening I had been adopted, my home had become Joey's home, and I began to learn the rudiments of otter psychology. There was, too, a great deal about the African clawless otter's topography that I had never quite grasped in my previous reading.

Joey was the handsomest otter I have ever seen. Most of the world's otter species are very similar in over-all appearance—brownish above, grading to silvery gray-brown beneath, with minor variations in the sharpness of gradation between the two colors. Joey had a glistening white bib, sharply delimited by the brown at the level of his eyes and ears and down the neck. Near his chest the white bib faded gradually to his belly color. His head was oddly shaped for an otter in that the muzzle was almost doglike, set off more sharply from the rest of the head than is usual for a *Lutra* otter, and he had a prominent deep-pink nose. But it was Joey's paws that really set him apart from the "typical" otters.

Joey's hands had the over-all effect of those of a soft pink, plastic doll, and the same was true of his hind feet. While most otters have extensive webs between the fingers and the toes, the degree of webbing varying with the species, Joey's webs were almost nonexistent, barely more functional than the "webs" that are visible between our own spread fingers. The fingers and toes of more typical otters bear stout claws, used only when needed, but African clawless otters, as their name suggests, lack claws on their hands as adults. In infancy small vestigial claws are present, but by the time Joey arrived he had lost all but the permanent nubs that would remain on the middle three toes of each hind foot—those he would use for scratching himself. Presumably the other claws have been discarded as the species evolved, not so much because they were not needed as because their continued presence (except on the three "grooming" toes) was in some way a disadvantage. Perhaps without claws each digit gained more space for nerve endings, increasing the sensitivity of the hands.

And how the little otter used those hands! He could manipulate a small object as dexterously as any raccoon—even more so—and his constant preoccupation with handling things went far beyond the play of other species of otter. He lived in a world of experience vastly more complex than the one in which Pixie skulked on four feet that were nothing more than feet, a world separated from the fox by more than a pair of doors.

For what seems now to have been a long time but was actually only a matter of days, I could not bring myself to trust Joey. Although he was still a cub his size was already considerable and he had most of his adult dentition. His teeth were formidable, and I still remembered his explosive snort and charge when I first peered at him in his crate at the airport. I did not then understand the otter mentality at all. The two otters I had had at home before, Ottie and Flump, were very young cubs, and sickly ones at that. Joey was my first big otter, and I believed in trusting no animal on such short acquaintance. Since then I have learned something of otters, but this knowledge came too late for Joey to benefit fully from it. My notebook for that first week mentions the otter's use of his teeth in play, but that his play "is not gentle enough to suit me." How much I had to learn! Although I scarcely realized it I was being initiated into the small fraternity of those who have felt the sharp teeth with which an otter so often gives expression to his abrasive affection. I took to wearing light leather gloves during our play periods and they saved my hands from most of the superficial scratches that came from Joey's stout but sharp canine teeth. The gloves proved useless against the pinching effect of the teeth, though, and I took action to reform the cub. After one particularly painful nip I cuffed him on the nose, saying "NO!" in the sternest voice I could muster, considering that I expected to be answered by a real bite. Joey didn't attack—in fact he seemed to take no notice of the blow. Following the next few nips I increased the force of my reprimand until he did notice, and thereafter a good blow would make him stop playing momentarily and resume with less gusto. In fact, after a cuff Joey forsook biting and limited himself to feinting strikes of the head with his mouth closed. For a while. One day, in the course of our rough-and-tumble activity I slapped Joey on the snout as usual and a moment later saw blood trickling from both nostrils. I had bloodied his nose. That such a tough little animal should have an Achilles heel so surprised and chagrined me that I let him get away with a few "free" nips, and kept future disciplinary slaps away from his nose.

Joey had learned about water while Dora had him, and the next time I ran water in the tub he froze instantly, but momentarily, into a rigidly alert posture, then dashed straight toward the tub. He had trouble getting into it, though, and would get hung up halfway over the top. I still respected those teeth and his person, so I refrained from what would have been a simple matter of boosting him over. Instead I hunted in the basement and produced a couple of scraps of plywood, which I arranged into a makeshift ramp propped between the toilet and the tub. The trouble was that Joey wanted to climb into the tub at the end where the tap flowed, and he used the ramp reluctantly only two or three times before he mastered the little half-jump that would get him hung up far enough astern to totter over the brink.

In those days I still slept in a conventional bed and it never

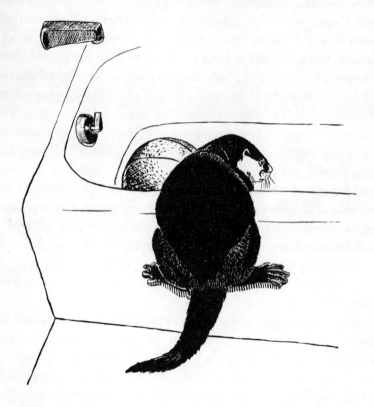

occurred to me that Joey might want to share it with me. For some reason it never occurred to Joey either (although sleeping in my bed was to be *de rigueur* for his successors). Joey slept in two places principally, under the dresser and under the bed. This latter location had disadvantages because he sometimes slept only partly under the bed and when I got up in the morning I had to be careful about where I set my feet. For the first few days the problem didn't exist, because Joey woke up inexplicably and began to prowl about at three o'clock in the morning. He tired early in the day and by midafternoon retired to one of his sleeping places, to be roused to activity only with difficulty. Dora's letters (and Maxwell's account of his own clawless otter, Edal, bore her out) indicated that Joey preferred a diurnal existence, undoubtedly because companionship was available only by day. In a flash of inspiration I opened an atlas and checked the world's time zones. As I had suspected, Joey was awakening on his old Liberian timetable, at the time when the Weyers would be getting up. Within a week Joey gradually adjusted himself to his new daily schedule and lived a totally diurnal existence.

Joey housebroke himself almost immediately, if not very conveniently. He chose the bedroom doorsill and returned to it with an almost religious zeal. I spread newspaper over the area after the first incident and Joey honored its limits, subject only to a foible that Dora had written about—sometimes only his front end covered the spread. Had Joey lived long enough he could doubtless have been taught to move his bowels in a better place, but he lived such a short time. Still, Joey did have one almost admirable trait, when it came to toilet training, that none of his successors had. He scrupulously avoided soiling the water in the tub. Normally, after leaving the tub Joey would scrootch and scrunch around on the bath mat to dry his fur, but when a call from nature came he climbed from the tub and lolloped over to the bedroom doorway, taking what seemed like half his bath water with him.

The end came slowly but certainly for the little clawless otter. Flump, the too-young South American cub, died a few days after Joey's arrival. She had not thrived from the first, and although I had no sure knowledge of the nature of her illness I had kept her physically isolated from him. Flump's symptoms suggested feline enteritis—cat distemper—from what I had read of it, but the disease had never been reported in an otter before. It, or a similar disease, had been found in mink—which are members of the same family, the Mustelidae—but the picture was further complicated by the fact that ferrets, also members of the family and closely related to the mink, do not contract the disease despite attempts to infect them experimentally in laboratories.

On the day Flump died the Zoo's vet was at home, so I performed a gross autopsy, which revealed lesions strongly suggestive of enteritis. The doctor made arrangements to have Joey immunized, but there was a problem with the vaccine. In the Zoo, cats and those other species known to be susceptible to feline enteritis are immunized when they arrive. The vaccine is perishable and is dated, and it is ordered as its need is anticipated. There was in stock, for this reason, only one vial of vaccine, two months past its expiration date. Since it was all there was, and a reorder would take time, and since the expiration dates normally allow for a safe time margin, the decision was made to administer it.

At eight o'clock on the morning of 16 February, the day after Flump's death, Bob Reville called to say he was on his way over to help move Joey. Thereupon I threw on a coat, went out to the car and started both the motor and the gasoline heater, to warm up the large, heavy, steel-framed monkey crate I had put in it the night before at the Zoo. When he arrived we carried the crate into the house and set it up in the doorway of my study, Joey's principal playroom. To my surprise the otter waddled into the crate with almost no hesitation, and meekly allowed me to drop the door. He snorted angrily when the cloth I draped over the wire-sided crate fluttered near, but he took the dash out to the Volkswagen and the drive to the Zoo uncomplainingly, and without the heavy panting characteristic of his species in fright.

At the Zoo hospital I let Joey out of the crate and he set about calmly exploring the corridor. I decided not to take part in restraining or injecting him for fear of having him associate me with a painful experience, a precaution that subsequent events showed to have been unnecessary; I just didn't know about otter cubs. Cosmo Barbetto, one of our best keepers, and another man approached the cub as he investigated the far end of the corridor and Cosmo, reaching quietly and slowly toward his neck, suddenly pinned Joey's head to the floor—how I don't know. The other keeper immobilized the cub's hindquarters. Joey struggled like a fury, snorting and snarling, then broke into the most piteous wail I have ever heard, the sound Dora had described. Instantly our nurse, Vinnie Martine, stepped up to the otter. Even as I watched the injection, which took mere seconds, seeing Vinnie's raven hair and crisp white uniform suspended over the writhing, screaming otter, my mind conjured up a fully formed image of the next event, of what would happen when the keepers released their hold on the otter. It was a vision incarnadined with blood.

Cosmo's anchor man let go first and stepped back. As the otter's struggles increased with his partial freedom, Cosmo released him and took a long stride backward too. Joey lunged at him with an explosive snort as I had anticipated, but that was all. He stopped as suddenly as he had begun, and relaxed. It was no trouble at all to lure him back into the crate with Cosmo's help (Joey seemed to have forgotten his indignity already) and take him home. For a couple of hours he was listless—a reaction to the vaccine—but by evening he was his old ebullient self again.

The next few days brought a portent of disaster, but in the false flush of confidence that my ignorance fostered I saw only the bright side of things. I had come to trust Joey much more than I had expected to, and we were caught up in the game of wits that is an otter-human relationship. Joey learned all of the subterfuges that meant I would attempt to leave him behind in the study. No longer could I roll his ball into a corner and expect him to galumph off after it—not even a stream of water from the bathtub tap would lure him away from the door when he sensed my departure, and that requires an almost super-lutrine degree of determination. The only thing that still worked (and I suspected that only a matter of time stood between this success and utter failure) was to offer him a chicken drumstick. As in Liberia, Joey's interest in the rest of the world evaporated in the presence of food. Pixie, isolated on the other side of the door, gave no sign of interest in the otter he never saw.

On the eighth day after his arrival I locked Joey in the bathroom to keep him from wrestling the broom as I swept the bedroom. My confidence that the water in the tub would keep him occupied shattered with the crash that sounded from the locked room. Joey had climbed, via the toilet seat, into the sink. The washbasin held all of the things I normally kept on the drainboard that surrounded it—the can of pressurized shaving soap, razor, hair tonic, and a cake of soap. The soap was bitten into several pieces, which would not fit back together to form the entire cake. Joey was clearly upset and apparently unable to solve the problem of getting to the floor again, so I helped him down and watched him carefully for the rest of the day. During the night he vomited on the bathroom floor a clear yellowish liquid with two or three bright green spots in it. It was not clear at the time that this was indeed vomitus, but it had to be, for through the worst of his illness, however pressing his intestinal pain, he always managed to reach his newspaper before he defecated; vomiting was alien to him, and he recognized no code of honor where it was concerned. Later in the day he seemed normal again, and played with a rubber ball and a Ping-pong ball, but any idea I had that he had reacted to swallowing some of the soap dissipated in the early evening, when he began to moan piteously several times and then threw up again. I offered him a drumstick and he carried it off, but later I found it uneaten, and saw more vomitus. In the meantime Joey had found a paper bag and crawled into it to sleep. Later he reappeared, lively as ever, and ate some raw chicken hearts, but they didn't stay down.

The following day Joey refused all food, although he drank water freely; he passed a loose, mucoid stool, whose black coloration meant that it contained his own digested blood. His vomiting became frequent and preceded by those horrible moans. He continued to play actively in the tub, but even the water he drank would not remain down. Against these symptoms of feline enteritis were other conditions that did not fit the pattern. His temperature, as far as I could tell, was not elevated and he was far from listless. Further, it was now nearly forty-eight hours since the onset of vomiting and, in cats, death should have occurred by that time. I tried to squirt some beef-liver broth into his mouth, with little luck. First I teased him into nipping at my gloved hand, and with his mouth open I got some liquid into it. His reaction was one of distaste. Subsequent attempts he greeted with gestures reminiscent of a human baby, which would have been comical under any less grim circum-

D

stances. When the rubber syringe approached his mouth Joey shook his head in a "No!" that was as anthropomorphic as it was emphatic. If I persisted, he then pushed the syringe away with his hands.

He had not yet lost too much weight. He had weighed eight pounds when he left Liberia and now weighed slightly more than that, but not nearly as much as he should have. He had periods of listlessness, but these alternated with periods of spirited play. He passed more tarry black stools. Before going to bed I offered him the white of a hard-boiled egg (one of his favorite foods), then a yolk. He didn't shy away from these, as he had from other foods, but he contented himself with treating them as toys, manipulating but not eating them. By morning he had eaten the egg yolk, for there were particles scattered near his bed and later, undigested, in his stool. Before I arose in the morning I could hear him handling his Ping-pong ball. Finding a bit of dried-out chicken in Joey's bed, I offered him some fresh pieces, but evidently his interest in the old meat had been only as an object to be fingered.

Late in the morning I reluctantly left for work. When I returned matters had worsened. Joey's diarrhea had become pinkish, with gray inclusions—bits of sloughed intestinal lining. The veterinarian had given me some injectible penicillin-streptomycin, and Bob Reville came over to help me administer it. It took a very heavy needle, both because of the viscosity of the medication and the toughness of the otter's hide, which had bent a stout 18-gauge needle during his vaccination. He resisted an oral intake of neomycin in a thick, yellowish suspension (those antibiotics were not intended to fight the virus, against which they would have no effect, but to ward off any secondary infection that might arise in his weakened system), and he objected only mildly to the injection. The nictitating membranes, the "third eyelids," which are small and apparently as functionless in an otter as in man, seemed to extend farther from the inner corners of Joey's eyes than before. I was to note this phenomenon in other otters as death approached, and the best guess I can make concerning its significance is that with the bodily dehydration that results from vomiting and diarrhea the otter's eyes bulged less and that in so doing more of the inner corners showed.

I am not dwelling upon the details of Joey's illness because I take some perverse pleasure in them; the truth is that in writing from notes that were intended to salvage at least a small bit of knowledge from a somber situation I have relived one of the most oppressive experiences of my life. The details are spread out here only in the hope of exposing, however sketchily, one of the least attractive sides of sharing life with a "good" wild animal.

A few minutes after midnight of the twenty-first I took stock of the situation. It was more than seventy-two hours since Joey began to vomit, and just over fifty-five hours since the throwing-up became frequent; forty-eight hours had passed since the first indication of diarrhea. In the entire period he had eaten about five chicken hearts and one hard-boiled egg yolk, and nothing more. His water intake was falling off now, most likely because even a drink triggered vomiting. For the past twenty-four hours Joey had been feeling feverish. The little otter was still small enough (and perhaps weakened enough) for me to be able to grasp him behind the ears with one hand. By lifting him until his forefeet were off the floor I was able to squirt about a teaspoonful of the neomycin suspension into his mouth—if his front paws touched the floor he was able to squirm effectively enough to make medication impossible. Twice again I managed to get an equal quantity of medicine into him. Later, as I drifted into sleep, I could hear Joey heave a deep sigh from time to time.

In the morning Joey played in the bathtub, and when he twisted his body the outline of his rib cage was very evident. He was losing flesh rapidly now. He continued to pass loose black stools and showed no interest in food; I continued to force medication into his mouth. His play was still fairly vigorous, and after each session in the tub he dried himself assiduously. Fortunately Joey still maintained a relatively high water-intake, replacing the liquids that escaped in his bowel movements (the latter, I discovered, occurred about an hour and a half after he drank, and I could predict them).

By the evening of the twenty-second his stools had lost their black color and were a clear yellow, sometimes with grayish, gelatinous inclusions. His interest in the world around him had not waned; during the day he pulled off two of the baseboard hot-air grills, which the previous owner of the house had never anchored to the wall. I gave him further doses of neomycin and added Kaopectate, then later got a little beef tea down his throat. Throughout the day Joey did not vomit, even after the broth, and he had few bowel movements. His weight had fallen to below seven pounds and his eyes had a flat, sunken look, with a large expanse of nictitating membrane showing. He was sinking fast, and in desperation I called Bob Reville to help me— despite Joey's now rapid dehydration he had begun to struggle against any liquids I tried to administer. The hour was midnight.

When Bob restrained him, the otter did not resist. We had just returned from a futile attempt to obtain some glucose for injection from the local hospital—the nurse would not summon the resident on duty, and I could think of no way to get around her. The fact that I was dressed in a sweat shirt and old trousers and had not shaved since the day before probably had not contributed anything in my favor. With Bob holding Joey I resorted to the drastic measure of squirting a quantity of warm water into the otter's rectum with a rubber ear-syringe, in the hope that the intestinal lining would absorb at least some of the liquid. Almost immediately Joey expelled the water with a small amount of fecal matter. Then we forced half an ounce of broth orally and I injected subcutaneously the little saline solution I had been able to find at an all-night drugstore. Joey was completely limp by this time. I held his head under the bathtub tap and he drank, but barely. Then I set him into a box lined with warm towels. At two in the morning Bob drove me back to the drugstore, where we had met and where I had left my automobile. A few minutes later I was home again. Joey was dead, his paws cool, and a liquid dripping from his mouth. Although I knew it would accomplish nothing I inserted a tube into his throat and attempted resuscitation by breathing into his lungs. At last I admitted defeat and almost numbly closed his mouth, but it came open again in a ghastly grimace. Thereafter, as I sat staring at the lifeless corpse, I experienced one of those terrible tricks of the senses—I saw small movements of Joey's chest, movements that did not really exist, even as a reflex of death.

The vet was not at the Zoo when I arrived, so, because it was a Friday and the tissues would have begun to break down by Monday, I performed a gross autopsy myself. The body, despite severe dehydration, still had a layer of subcutaneous fat perhaps a quarter of an inch thick. The intestines showed no signs of inflammation—perhaps a recovery from the enteritis had been under way, and death resulted from some secondary cause—but the lungs were bloody in areas. I saved and preserved parts of the various internal organs, but pathologists were unable to make any conclusive diagnosis from them.

In spite of my having seen Joey's death rictus and having probed through his innards, my most vivid memory of his last day was not of those times, but of a poignant scene that took place a few hours earlier. A khaki shirt had fallen from the dresser to the floor the day before, and Joey had adopted it for his bed. A few hours before he died he lay upon this shirt, his life tenuous and fleeting, hardly able to lift his head at my voice. One of his small pink doll's hands weakly but deliberately caressed and fingered a fold of the shirt.

4   Fox and Hounds

       Uneasiness grasps me as I consider how to introduce Goop, and later Beever and Mimsy. I must refer to Goop as "my next otter," but I cannot without sounding too much like Browning's Duke of Ferrara. In less than a year and a half I had attended the deaths of three otters, and two others died in my absence. From a dispassionate point of view their deaths were not in vain—prevention and treatment of the disease that killed them are not one hundred percent effective, but are high, and others may now live because of the knowledge. But my personal feelings of loss at the otters' deaths are deeper than I dare admit. Each one was a unique, valiant little spirit whose passing I would have sacrificed anything to prevent.

       Three weeks elapsed between Joey's death and Goop's arrival (from the same dealer who sold Flump to me). In the interim I scrubbed the house as thoroughly as I could, and hoped that enough time had passed to render harmless any remaining virus (if it *was* a virus). Living without an otter proved to be worse than living with one, and I was anxious to have things get back to abnormal as quickly as possible.

The small otter was delivered to me at the Zoo in a cardboard carton on 15 March, 1962. He clambered out of the box, chittering, and allowed me to hold him—albeit squirmily—water him, and transfer him to a wooden crate in which he remained,

protesting, until I opened it again at home, three hours later. He was undoubtedly a Colombian otter, but I could never be completely certain because he had rubbed his nose raw in the original crate en route to the dealer's and had a large pink scab that obliterated the nose pattern he had been born with. He played in the bathtub, drank his fill in it, and devoured a good portion of boiled chicken. Then he sprawled out on the bath mat in front of the hot-air register and fell asleep. When he awoke Goop was a dynamo. He played for a little while with a

Ping-pong ball, but abandoned it as soon as he discovered that he could wrestle with my hand and, like Joey, he bit too roughly for my taste. Although he weighed in the neighborhood of a mere five pounds, he had most of his adult dentition. When the bites became too painful, as inevitably they did, I clouted him on the side of his head, as I had done with Joey, but again I began by underestimating his pain threshold, and it took time to build up the force of the blow until it carried a message other than "this is part of our game." Not that he ever uttered a yelp of pain at being struck, but he did come to recognize a slap as chastisement. Several times when the play grew rough I managed to slip one of Goop's hind feet into his mouth and found to my surprise that he bit down just as hard on himself, as nearly as I could tell, as he had done on me, without showing the least sign of pain. For a short time Goop considered any portion of my limbs as a fair target in the game and until he learned the meaning of "NO!" it was necessary to take drastic measures to keep him from sinking his teeth merrily into the soft flesh in the crook of my arms. The only tactic that worked involved throwing him to the floor. A trip through the air of about three feet with a drop of about eighteen inches may sound like a cruel and inhumane punishment, but it was not. I threw Goop so that he would land, feet down, on a rug and, to be honest about it, I kept my hands on him as he dropped the first foot. Upon landing he usually ambled off elsewhere, with a look of hurt feelings. That look, which may sound like the most flagrant of anthropomorphisms in print, is a real phenomenon, and anyone who has ever been on intimate terms with an otter will know what I am talking about. I can't really describe it except to say that the otter has a way of looking up while keeping his head low, so that the white shows along the undersides of his eyes. Whatever its effect in nature on another otter, it has the devastating result of making me feel like an overbearing swine.

Goop had a bit more devilment in him than any other otter I have known before or since. He surprised me one evening, well after he had learned about "NO!," by disregarding the command. He had been chomping down more painfully than usual, and had one of my fingers, not in that toothless space immediately behind his canine teeth which was the least painful place for it to be, but held instead between his blade-like carnassials. I shouted prohibition, but instead of releasing me, this time he rolled his eyes upward, regarding me with intense curiosity, and increased the pressure of his jaws ever so slightly. This earned him a sterner "NO!" and a clout; he discovered what he had sought, that he couldn't get away with it, and that was that.

The one deterrent to Goop's pestering that always worked was a puff of cigarette smoke, and when he forgot to nip me with restraint I learned to draw in a mouthful of smoke and expel it in his face. The temporary smarting sensation in his eyes and nose he found distasteful, and he responded to it by diving from the sofa and running off. Goop was quick to learn, and after a few such reprimands he grew so cautious that when I lit up a cigarette he galumphed off to the opposite end of the sofa, despite my innocent intent. I could coax him onto my lap then, but if a big cloud of smoke passed over him (I had to learn to turn my head away while exhaling) he dove to the floor. But he never did connect the smoke with his hard biting; the smoke was something to be avoided on its own merits. Still, a week later, as I was lighting up, the little otter showed great interest in the flame. Foolishly, I held the lighter to see his reaction. With none of the legendary animal fear of fire Goop inched forward until, before I realized what was happening, he lunged slightly at the flame and in one fluid motion leaped away with a squawk. The smell of burnt hair and a close inspection showed that he had suffered nothing more than a couple of singed whisker tips, but thereafter my experimental ardor cooled somewhat.

Goop spent more time with me on the sofa than any of the other otters, and was the only one to fall asleep regularly at my side, rather than under the sofa or some other piece of furniture. Several times he climbed up on the bolster behind me and did something that could only have been a sign of affection; he half licked, half sucked in my ear or at the nape of my neck. It was, I believe, the same action I have seen other otters and Goop perform upon parts of their own bodies, principally paws and chest skin, a kind of grooming.*

For some reason "figure-eight" harnesses are almost impossible to obtain in the New York area, at least at the stores I'm familiar with; only later, when I met Dotty Wisbeski, who owned an otter too and seemed to know of an inexhaustible source of supply of the double-loop harnesses, did fitting one on an otter cease to be impossible and become merely impracticable. I should have known better, but I bought a standard dog harness for Goop, one of those contraptions that buckle under the chest, behind the forelegs, and have a nonadjustable strap that circles over the shoulders and forward at the juncture of neck and chest. From my attempts to harness Goop I learned something about otters, and the degree to which they rely upon the tactile information gathered by their sensitive whiskers. These whiskers, or vibrissae as they are technically called, are in fact one of the major achievements of mammals, and they are

* My studies since this time have convinced me that social grooming plays a part in the lives of otters nearly as important as it is to those celebrated "nit-pickers," the monkeys.

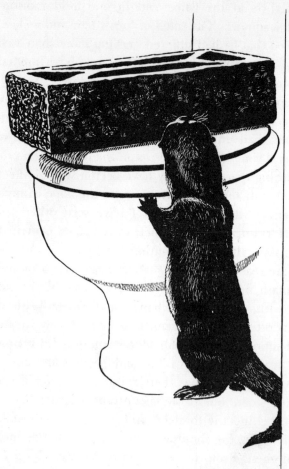

prominently developed in the majority of species. They are organs of touch par excellence, loosely comparable to the wire "curb feelers" sometimes attached to automobiles. In otters the vibrissae are arranged in five paired clusters. First and most prominent are two broad fields of bristles on the muzzle, the mystacial vibrissae, so called because they appear as a mustache below and to the sides of the nose. They inform the otter of anything tangible as much as two or three inches in front of his nose, and are probably very useful when he tackles a crayfish, keeping him posted on the whereabouts of the flailing pincers. Just behind the corners of the mouth are two more pairs of whisker patches, the genal, or cheek, vibrissae. The fish that slips past an otter's questing jaws will not escape should it brush the cheek whiskers. Other clusters, of a few bristles each, are located above and behind the eyes, and below the chin, serving to protect the otter from potential injury to its eyes and throat. Touch an otter's sensitive vibrissae without warning (or, for that matter, *with* warning in most cases) and his head whips around instantly to trap your finger in his jaws. A harness suffers the same fate.

Eventually Goop's phenomenal agility outdid itself. Time after time I maneuvered the harness over his head, but somehow it always ended up clenched in his teeth. The cub behaved as if we were playing a delightful new game, and always, as the leather brushed his vibrissae, he reacted with instant reflexes and pinpoint accuracy. This session taught me what I have come to regard as the most valuable lesson in otter-human relations—you can do almost anything with or to an otter if you make a game of it. I have been able to accomplish such Herculean tasks as claw trimming and administering medication by applying this technique; the problem (and it is a large one) lies in having only two hands instead of three, or preferably four. A minimum of two hands is necessary to keep the otter occupied, and the others for accomplishing the task at hand.

With perseverance I succeeded in ramming the harness over Goop's head once, and with further dogged effort managed to buckle it. In a twinkling his supple forelegs thrust upward between the neck strap and his neck, and moving like an amoeba within his skin, Goop had the harness slung about his midsection. He might have been able to extricate himself, but his discomfort seemed to indicate action on my part. Removing the harness proved to be more difficult than putting it on, mostly because the otter was beginning to be upset as the game lost its aspect of pleasure. But I did get the thing off, and the entire episode with its hint of panic must have left Goop's mind, for seconds later he was playing with the harness by himself. Thereupon he squirmed into the thing of his own accord, except that he went into it from the wrong end and got stuck. He lolloped off then from room to room, wedged firmly into his unwanted girdle. But this time he took matters a bit more calmly after a while, and stopped every so often to flop over on his side and toy with the dangling straps. Naturally, being an otter, he eventually wriggled free of his fetters.

For the first three days Goop and Pixie did not meet and I made no effort to introduce them, chiefly because I could not predict the fennec's reaction to an otter—he and Joey had never met. On the two or three occasions when I let the otter out into the living room Pixie stayed out of sight. Most of the time I played with Goop in my study, with the idea of withholding full house privileges until he formed strong toilet habits. The otter cub dogged my heels frantically wherever I went, and locking him in the study was a problem until I remembered Dora Weyer's trick. A dish of food took his mind off all else, allowing me to slip through the doorway unheeded. Out in the living room Goop seemed to be totally unaware of the fox's presence; if he picked up the fennec's scent he gave no sign of curiosity about it; but by the third day Pixie's curiosity reached the breaking point, and as silently as he had melted into the furniture he reappeared. Whenever the otter paused near suitable cover such as the sofa, I would have a fleeting view of Pixie, ears pricked forward, darting up erratically to sniff at Goop's tail, then disappearing again.

The extreme myopia of otter cubs may explain in part why Goop, like my first otter Ottie, was a foot-worshipper; one's feet are normally the most visible part of one's anatomy to a cub. Be that as it may, when Goop did catch sight of Pixie the fennec's anonymity came to an abrupt and humiliating end. Pix had sneaked up for another sniff when he caught the otter's eye. Goop whipped around. Pixie beat a hasty retreat. Goop, his stubby legs working for all they were worth, lumbered after him. Now no otter could hope to match speed on land with a long-limbed fox, but the cards were stacked against the fennec. On sand, soil, or rock the fennec would have been master of the situation, but on floor tile, not so. Pixie could trot with ease on tile, but when he attempted a fast getaway his wildly scrabbling feet got him nowhere for the first moments, and the more desperately he tried the less effective were his attempts. The otter's broad, rubbery, padded feet, on the other hand, admirably suited for traction, enabled him to keep pace, nearly, with his unwilling newfound playmate. In addition Goop (and his successor) quickly assimilated the art of cutting the fox off. The living room is L-shaped, one leg of which—the one that abuts the kitchen—serves as a dining area. The sofa is located along the inner wall of the other leg of the complex, commanding a limited view.

I was seated on the sofa when the two animals went dashing off. Rather than disturb whatever interplay might be taking place I sat quietly, stifling my curiosity as best I could, until from around the corner there burst forth a piercing cacophony in which I detected a fugue of the fennec's shrill rasping yap and the otter's metallic mélange of chuckles, chirps, and growls, uttered almost simultaneously, like some demoniac bagpipe. I had never heard the otter's sound before, but the fennec's yap was familiar enough—he was being attacked; he had hurled this same invective at me on the few occasions when I tried to corner him. Even before I reached the corner I could see in my mind the patches of fur and blood marking the battle site.

What I saw with my eyes was a crouching fox, ears laid back, lips retracted in the awful grimace of a cornered dog, and the otter sprawled languorously on his back, undulating very

slightly and very slowly, one forepaw extended toward the yapping fennec just beyond his reach. What made the scene utterly ridiculous was that the cornered fennec crouched out in the middle of the floor, yards from the nearest corner. Until the chase began again the two continued their duet.

That was the turning point in my relationship with otters, or more properly the first of two major milestones. I regret to this day that I did not trust Joey more, that up until his last days I trusted him only as long as I could see his every move. I had isolated him from the fennec because I did not relish having to thrust my hands into any melee of snapping jaws that might develop. I had insulted his good nature by underestimating it.

Goop and Pixie were never good companions, but only because the fox refused the otter's overtures. They played often, sometimes at Pixie's instigation, more often at Goop's, but the fennec seemed always to enter into the game of fox and hounds (Goop played the part of all the hounds) complainingly, with snarls and yaps, even when he himself had begun it. The chase would take them everywhere, until Goop had his fox at bay.

Pixie's safety zone for a while was the chair that served as his bed, and the first few times that Pix leaped up to safety Goop galumphed onward under the chair, not yet aware that his quarry was no longer ahead of him. But it wasn't long before Goop caught on to Pixie's ruse and thereafter he hauled himself up onto the chair in hot pursuit, leaving the fox no choice but to leap off again for another round. Another trick of Goop's was chasing the fennec past the corner where Pix's litter box was located. Invariably Pixie dashed along the two legs of the corner, and invariably the otter ran the hypotenuse, closing the gap. But Goop came to understand a certain tone to Pixie's snarl that meant the game was over, and he respected it.

On 22 March, a week after his arrival, Goop slept more often and longer than usual, and I laid this to my having been home all day playing with him when he wanted it, giving him a more strenuous day than he was accustomed to. Otherwise he was as alert as ever, and when he gnawed on my hands he did it with the reckless abandon I had come to expect. Shortly thereafter he tested the closed bedroom doors and discovered a new world. Although his depredations were minor and hardly worth mentioning I had not yet arrived at a state of total surrender and took measures to prevent another incursion. I remembered reading that black pepper will discourage investigation of forbidden areas by animals, so I dusted the doorsill liberally and went about my business. Later in the evening a volley of explosive sneezes confirmed the efficacy of the pepper barrier. I couldn't help smiling at the picture of Goop's surprise, although I sympathized with his distress. Suddenly the sneezing stopped and in a few minutes out waddled the otter, soaked from the shoulders forward. His water bowl was too small for him to have immersed so much of himself in it, which left only the toilet bowl as his watering place. I looked, and sure enough I had neglected to lower the cover. A few days later I found the pepper can, which I had kept handy, lying on its side in a corner, at the end of a long, tortuous trail of pepper grains.

Goop, I can only presume, had learned to hold his breath while playing with the new toy.

A week later I entered the bedroom one afternoon to find him sprawled on the bed. My bed. My sacrosanct bed. I do, or rather did, draw the line at this sort of familiarity from a wild animal, but Gavin Maxwell's account of the docility of otters he had permitted to sleep on his bed weakened my resolve, and I decided to take a chance and let him stay. Instead of the night-shirt I usually wore, I donned a pair of less comfortable ski pajamas with elastic cuffs on the legs and sleeves, because, however much I had come to trust the cub, a primeval apprehension for my bodily integrity gnawed at me, and the bottom-less nature of the nightshirt made it at the moment more a garment of vulnerability than comfort. Hopefully, I watched Goop squirm into the folds of the nightshirt, which I had left draped over the blanket for that purpose, but no sooner had I turned out the light than he burrowed under the blanket. I made a brief but fervent prayer to Saint Francis of Assisi to protect the otter from my flailing feet—and me from toothy retaliation—and then lay awake to await what might happen. Not much later Goop began to hump up like an inchworm and pulled out the sheet at the foot of the bed. Then I felt some-thing sharp on my ankle—probably a claw—and that did it. I was not disposed to lie awake all night waiting for the worst, so I banished him and barricaded the door with a concrete block. He scratched and chittered at the door for the better part of half an hour, then quieted.

Death was more merciful to Goop than it had been to Joey. It took him sooner, and with somewhat less pain, judging from his behavior. Goop ate his last regular meal on the evening of 29 March, exactly two weeks after he came to live with me. Late in the evening of the next day he suddenly leaped down from the sofa where he had been resting next to me, and ran in haste to a corner, uttering a strange, small sound. Then he ran aimlessly back and forth and vomited. For the next day he drank more often than usual and vomited several times, preceding each attempt with a squall of distress not at all like Joey's moan. Otherwise he was as playful as ever, although the play sessions were separated by longer intervals of sleep. He slept alternately under the bedroom dresser and in the bathtub. Although his eyes bulged normally, lacking the sunken look that accompanies dehydration from enteritis, by 1 April his rib cage jutted out in contrast to his sunken abdomen. On the preceding night Goop was asleep in the folds of my nightshirt again, and I let him stay. All night he was quiet but restless, sleeping next to my pillow, under the sheet next to my feet and between them, and at places between these extremes. I slept fitfully until half past six, when I had to get up for Sunday Mass before driving to the Zoo, where I was to be Officer of the Day.

I stayed up later than usual that night. Before retiring at one o'clock I was able to persuade Goop to drink some very diluted evaporated milk in warm water, and by spooning it into his mouth, rather than trying to squirt it in, administered a teaspoonful of neomycin-kaolin solution to him without any resistance. As before, I allowed him to sleep with me, figuring that the psychological comfort it afforded him might help him to fight the disease. Goop spent an uneasy night, and my own sleeplessness made me aware of his continual movements. Two or three times he left the bed to defecate, but always he returned to seek in vain for relief. At last I fell asleep. I vaguely remember the wake-up service's call at seven o'clock and the alarm clock ringing, but the lack of sleep took its toll, and I did not awaken fully until ten. Goop was not in bed. I called, but he gave no answer. He was lying on his side in the bathtub in an attitude of sleep. I debated awakening him until I saw that he wasn't breathing, and when I touched him his body was rigid. His eyes were closed and his posture indicated that he had died peacefully in his sleep. Only afterward did I recall the sound I had heard twice in my half-sleep. It was a soft cry, something like the call of a screech owl, tremulous, descending in volume and pitch. It was a whimper of distress that, to a human ear at least, carried a sound of suffering and weakness and, if I may be forgiven for an unjustifiable human interpretation, a sound of hopelessness. I have heard another otter make this sound since, apparently in a bad dream, but I hope I will never hear it again.

5   Skirts and Avocado

The cause of Goop's death was never determined with certainty; his autopsy, like Joey's, had been inconclusive. Wrapped in the ignorance that follows from a smattering of knowledge in a field outside my competence, I still had a strong hunch that a virus was the lethal agent, and almost as strong a feeling that the virus of feline enteritis, or something very similar to it, was the actual cause. Later events indicated that the hunch was right, but it had been without any solid proof to back it up.

In the meantime I did what I could in the wake of Goop's death to prevent a future occurrence. The house received a thorough scrubbing and airing, and I waited a longer period— over two months—before looking for another otter. I confess that no thought of any other kind of animal fluttered even momentarily through my mind. That a form of enteritis had afflicted and killed the three otters was beyond question, but enteritis is merely a word that describes symptoms. The *New Gould Medical Dictionary* defines the term as "Any intestinal tract inflammation, acute or chronic," and it may result from any of a number of causes. Poison was a remote possibility, but I could rule it out because Flump had lived her brief life in a box, consuming only milk. Bacterial infection was a serious possibility, however, for otters normally eat only freshly killed flesh and Pixie in true fox-fashion always cached uneaten food, frequently in his litter box, to be eaten later—sometimes days later. Goop might have found and consumed such a moldy bit of meat in the box and, for that matter, since Pix had had prior access to the room in which Joey lived, the otter could have come upon a very old cache, too. Such old meat, harmless to the fennec, could easily be lethal to an otter cub too young to know enough to leave it alone. But I put little faith in such a likelihood, again because of Flump, and because I had learned the hard way that my otters were the most fastidious of eaters. That enteritis could have been the product of mechanical abrasion from the cubs' having swallowed some sharp objects was unlikely too, because wild otters normally ingest quantities of things with sharp edges. The chitinous shells of crayfish and other crustaceans and the bones and scales of fish regularly appear in quantity in a wild otter's feces, and in fact I have seen on rocks old spraints that were composed solely of such particles, the soft material having been leached away by rains. The spraints, or stools, of otters, when fresh, contain a large amount of mucoid material, which must be secreted by the gut precisely for the purpose of protecting itself from sharp edges.

That left a virus as the last possibility. Most likely it had been in Flump when she arrived and had passed to Joey either by air or on my clothing. Goop might have had it on arrival or he might have come into contact with some bit of vomitus or feces that our cleaning had missed. There existed also a remote chance that Pixie might be an asymptomatic carrier of the disease. Some diseases are transmitted in this fashion—gnus from South Africa, for example, can carry, and transmit to domestic cattle, a disease called malignant head catarrh without ever showing a sign of the disease themselves. If Pixie were the vector I would, I decided, have to choose whether I would have fennecs or otters in the future, but that was a matter for later consideration. I would, however, isolate any new otter from Pixie for a month.

Such were the thoughts that occupied my mind in the months after the passing of Goop. Friends urged me to abandon the idea of getting another otter in the near future, until the true nature of the disease was known. The unsentimental side of my nature held sway in the long run, the part of me which realized that without persistence and another attempt the identity of the disease might never come to light. It isn't difficult to gamble the life of a hypothetical animal yet of the future—and my hunch pointed the way to eliminate much of the hazard. When I called the animal dealer, the time elapsed since Goop's death had already exceeded by several weeks the known potential span of infectibility of the virus of feline enteritis outside a living animal. I had another hunch (which subsequent events have satisfied me was right) that the dealer's premises harbored the virus, infecting new arrivals, so I made it a condition of my order that the otter be brought to the Zoo directly from the airport, without a stopover at his establishment. This he agreed to, and I was reassured by the knowledge that a former keeper from my department now working with him could be trusted to abide by my condition. Then I waited. Some animal dealers today are little more than traffickers in living meat, whose concern for their merchandise is limited to ordering enough individuals in excess of their wants to allow for the usual (but for the most part avoidable) mortality in transit, and to keeping their animals alive long enough to sell them. This dealer was fortunate in having with him a man who had worked well in a zoo and whose concern for the animals went beyond the commercial aspect. In fairness to the dealer I must admit that he followed my advice and sent hyper-immune serum to his contact in Colombia (by the time Beever arrived I knew of at least a dozen otters of his that had died in the same way), but the serum required refrigeration, and he later reported ruefully that the Colombian compound never bothered to refrigerate its serum.

Beever arrived in early July. He was brought to the Zoo directly from Idlewild Airport as stipulated, without a visit to the dealer's place. He was a friendly little thing, eager to crawl all over me, but it was early afternoon and I wasn't able to take him home immediately. Instead, he spent the rest of the afternoon in a carrying crate (the one he came in was small and by now filthy). Joe Ruf, head keeper of the Mammal Department, spent more time out of his office that afternoon than usual, and I could hardly blame him in view of the shrill, impatient chittering that issued from the crate. From the Zoo I took the cub directly to my newly found veterinarian Dr. Wolf, in a neighboring town, where he received a prophylactic injection of cat serum to protect him against feline enteritis.

The drive from the Zoo to the veterinarian's office in New Jersey was far from uneventful. The cub bit me. We had just crossed the George Washington Bridge and were heading north on the Palisades Interstate Parkway. The cub was in his crate beside me on the front seat. Since we left the Zoo he had kept up an increasing chittering of complaint that was unbearable in the already noisy interior of my Volkswagen. I then had the station-wagon model known as the Kombi, which had only a front seat and lacked any interior lining. Ordinarily the noise of the motor was all but overpowering, with nothing inside to absorb the sound, and the bare metal walls and roof did things to the otter's cries that made them seem to originate inside my skull, like the sound of a pond full of spring peepers.

A few years before, I had driven ten thousand miles, through Washington and California and back to New York, with an

unweaned skunk, and part of the time he had been content to crawl under my shirt and sleep away the miles. It occurred to me that the otter might do the same thing. The traffic was moderate just north of the bridge, so I leaned over and opened the front of the crate in the moving car. The otter immediately lurched out of his prison and wobbled toward me, his voice stilled at last, and came to rest at my side. By this time the car had slowed appreciably, as my attention divided itself between the road and the otter, and I reached for the stick to shift down to third gear. In fourth gear the stick is pulled back near the seat, and as I reached down for the stick I felt a sudden stabbing pain in one of the fingers on my right hand. The little otter had reacted quite naturally to the sudden unfamiliar movement inches from his face by snapping at it. To make matters worse, by this time we had come upon a feeder lane from Route 9W, so that the Volkswagen was now traveling in three lanes of suddenly dense traffic. I dared not take my eyes off the road again. Somehow I scooped the otter up in my right hand, deposited him back in the crate, and closed it. Bombarded by renewed chittering, I drove for the next fifteen minutes or so unable to examine my wound, but knowing that there was a deep gash spurting blood in copious quantities. There is a stop sign at the end of the exit ramp that abuts Route 9W, and I did at last find the opportunity to survey the damage. It was a good thing that the stop gave me time, because I needed it to find the microscopic, bloodless pinprick the cub had left.

Two months later Beever inflicted his second, and only other, bite upon me. He was resting under the sheet of my bed, a new habit, when I poked him. He came out like a shot and we roughhoused for a while. During this play I must have touched a sensitive spot, for his head whipped around and his teeth closed on my hand. I let out a yelp—although his teeth had not broken my skin, the bite hurt—but even before my reflexes translated the pain into voice Beever had loosened his hold and pulled away. A painful nip deserves some form of chastisement, to lessen the chance of a recurrence, but I found myself unable to mete out any punishment. Beever was lying there prostrate, his eyes upturned, with an expression on his face—actually with his entire body in a posture—that bespoke anguish. I am in no way guilty of an anthropomorphism when I say this: the otter was without question suffering a pain as real as a physical blow. He seemed to be waiting for me to strike him. Naturally I didn't add a physical blow to his pyschological one; in fact, it took me several minutes of reassuring talk and stroking before he rose from his state of withdrawal, and his first tentative, almost delicate, nip when he began once again to play filled me with a very real joy. Maxwell's otter, Mijbil, once underwent a similar spasm of remorse, except that his bite had been a deliberate one.

Because of the possibility that Pixie was the innocent vector of the deadly enteritis that had destroyed the other cubs, I was still keeping Beever quarantined in the otter half of the house— the complex of study, bedroom, and bath—and limited Pix to his usual haunts in the other half. Three weeks had been the previous danger period, and I allowed another week to be safe; Beever was still in perfect health.

On the August day when the meeting was to take place I took the safe course that I had followed often in the past. I locked Beever in his traveling cage, a rather large affair with widely spaced bars. Many other animal handlers forgo such a precaution (in fact, I had often forgone such controlled introductions in the Zoo with no more mishap than when I did use a wire or barred screen) but I decided to play it safe. With Beever thus under control I opened the door to the study and waited for Pixie's curiosity to win over his wariness. He skulked silently under the table in sight of the doorway for a few brief moments, then trotted directly to the cage. Not a bit of caution did he show, none of the mincing back and forth that I expected of a fennec investigating something new. Instead he trotted matter-of-factly over to the cage and the two animals stood briefly nose-to-nose in what seemed to me to be an unusually amiable fashion for a first encounter. The possibility exists, of course, that Beever was displaying the innocent amiability of a very young cub, and that Pixie acted under the influence of his experiences with Goop, but more likely another explanation fits the situation better. The louvered double doors between the rooms were a very poor fit. They closed unevenly, and the pair that divided the otter's half of the house from the fennec's cleared the floor by not less than half an inch. It seems more than likely that the otter and fennec had been getting acquainted olfactorily via the space under the door ever since Beever's arrival, and that their visual introduction was an anticlimax.

Pixie formed the same sort of relationship with Beever that he had with Goop. There were wild chases accompanied by sounds appropriate to the lower reaches of hell, but never any bloodshed. The fennec seemed always to wind up on the short end of the encounter, but despite his show of irritation he often initiated the chases, and afterward continued to skulk up behind the otter. And although he still snarled at Beever when cornered, his demeanor then was much more relaxed than it had been with Goop.

Their encounters were frequent and soon fell into a pattern. Beever was the dominant animal, not because he had ever trounced his companion, but probably because of his larger size and improbably superior maneuverability. The proof of this came in a series of very strange encounters. They were strange because they involved two most dissimilar creatures following protocols of their own kind, and yet each seemed to be "satisfied" with the proceedings. I don't pretend to any great knowledge of either fennec or otter behavior, but I think the interpretations of the facts are valid ones. Pixie was lying upright in the middle of the floor in the pose of the stone lions at the entrance to the New York Public Library. Beever shuffled over to him and pushed his muzzle into one of the fennec's cavernous ears, like some gros. bumblebee probing into a flower. Pixie held still during the investigation, even when the otter reached out with his paw to pull the ear closer. In a little while Beever tired of his occupation and ambled off; Pixie never moved. There is evidently some significance to a fennec in ear-poking, for I had seen Pixie give another fennec the same treatment. Evidently, too, the submissive response of the fox had a meaning among his own species—a hostile or even a nervous fox will not allow his person to be so searched. That Pixie's immobility was not due to fear was demonstrated in one of the later reoccurrences of the act by the way he tolerated not only the ear-pulling but a complete going-over of his person, and the way he moved his head when Beever sniffed at his nose, his jowls, ears, and other facial areas, like a man responding to the tactile adjustments of a barber's hands. Any similar liberties on my part would have been met by the fennec's teeth while he cringed in a totally different posture with his ears laid flat along his neck.

Of what significance the procedure was to the otter I don't know. Some tame otters I have seen liked to nuzzle into a human ear, but this is as far as I can go. Is there a scent gland in the fennec's ear that brings a message to another fennec (and is merely an interesting odor to an otter)? Beever's use of his paws is understandable enough—a friendly meeting of two otters involves such pawing. Another remarkable aspect of this play is the restraint Beever practiced. When playing with me Beever, like all other otters, seemed never to know his own strength—that is to say, the strength of his jaws. He needed continual

reminders from me in the form of verbal and manual rebukes to refresh his memory and soften his bite. With the fennec, on the other hand, he seemed to be extraordinarily gentle. The jaws that could drive their teeth through a leather boot in anger or leave a livid welt on my arm in play might easily have, by oversight, snapped Pixie's spindly limbs like chicken bones, but Pix never so much as yelped. By the end of a year, when the two animals parted for the last time, the only evidence of wear and tear that Pixie could show was a bedraggled tail-tip. Beever had learned to clamp his teeth on the fox's brush, and as Pix scrabbled wildly to escape, little by little he caused the plucking of his tail. I suppose that I'm more pro-otter than pro-fennec, but I can't resist the temptation to point out that if Pixie had held still when Beever grabbed him he would not have lost even a hair.

Beever's attitude toward humans underwent a series of changes. Although at first I was just another member of the race of humans who he had come to understand meant him no harm and could fulfill his innate need for companionship, our relationship grew rapidly into a strong personal one. I suppose it was the product of a combination of circumstances, some of them external to the otter, but he seemed to me to have a benevolent spirit that transcended the natural otter eudaemonism (I beg to be forgiven for the use of the last word, but it is doubly appropriate, both in its proper meaning and as a pun). Perhaps Joey and Goop would have been as good, had they lived, but Beever did live to young adulthood, and did keep his total good will all the while.

By now I am used to being referred to by my friends as "Mother" when I have assumed the task of bottle-rearing a young animal, but the term always raises some vague irritation within me; I resent the implication the more because in most cases the duty has devolved upon me only when I was unable to find a woman who could be counted upon to channel her inborn maternal inclinations to the task. I confess that on occasion I have felt stirrings of what must be paternal solicitude over a young animal or pride in its accomplishment but I daresay I wouldn't recognize a motherly urge if it did arise.

Still, like it or not, a parent-offspring relationship does exist when you rear an animal. Presumably it regards you as its mother, regardless of your sex, if you are the provider of milk and protection; how long the parental image remains, either in its original form or transmuted into a trusted-companion image, depends upon the species involved. It dissolves rapidly with maturity in those animals, like skunks, which live solitary lives in adulthood. In an otter the parent-cub status probably persists for a while after the family breaks up as a unit, but just as likely an amiable recognition persists for a long time, maybe permanently, if one can believe some written accounts. The otter recognizes his human one-time foster parent as the dominant companion, at any rate.

During our first week I took a few days off (a practice I had been following in lieu of a formal vacation) and took Beever out on the lawn often. On those days he accorded anyone who approached a friendly welcome, but on one day (perhaps some internal condition was the cause) he challenged my hand as I played with him. I stopped its movement instantly and waited to see if a bite would follow, but he calmed down almost immediately and our play continued. Later in the day he challenged me again as I entered his half of the house, but a sniff at my shoe reassured him, and he never again behaved this way toward me. A comical sidelight of that morning on the lawn occurred when a titmouse, whose call has something of the timbre of the otter's chirp, was drawn by his call and stayed for a long time, in a state of perplexity, I'm sure, in a nearby tree.

Dorothy Reville drove me home from work on an early August day when I had left my car at the repair shop, and her meeting with Beever set a pattern for his future encounters with women. Until that time, when I came home Beever seemed unaware of my arrival until I unlatched the door to his half of the house. This evening he heard us talking and immediately set up his chirping "rally" call until I let him out. Dorothy had on a wide skirt with large patches of varied colors, and plainly it upset the little otter. He tensed and "Hah-ed" at her—his call that signaled a semihostile "who-goes-there" message. I brought him out on the lawn but he stayed at my feet chirping, and when I tried to lure him over to Dorothy by

walking past her he gave her a wide berth. This was to be his reaction to all skirts, and it really raised a problem when he met Dotty Wisbeski, who is addicted to full, flouncy-skirted dresses. Soon I found it necessary to prescribe slacks for all female visitors. (Both Dorothys, by the way, are nicknamed Dotty, and I use the more formal designation Dorothy for Mrs. Reville to avoid confusion as the two of them pass through the narrative from time to time.)

Our lives grew slowly more hermitlike with time, principally because those of my friends who could be counted upon to enjoy, or at least tolerate, a boisterous otter personality lived long distances away, and for me to visit them meant imposing solitude on Beever for more than the ten hours he now endured. I had not reckoned with the obvious fact that as Beever saw fewer people he would cease to regard them as a normal part of his environment and instead treat all strangers with suspicion. The only person he behaved civilly toward, in fact, was my next-door neighbor, whom he had met a few weeks earlier, while he was still friendly toward all humans.

Ruth and Wally Lindquist, new friends from another town who had had a series of skunks that ranged from docile to savage, and now had a pair of ferrets, paid us a visit in September. At first Beever treated them warily, then with occasional interludes of friendly approach. His reserved cordiality was short-lived, though, and after about half an hour he began to growl his low, menacing *"yeaaaaar"* that came to signal the end of his patience with a stranger. The Lindquists were familiar enough with animals to take Beever's outburst with good grace. Undaunted, they invited us to their home a few miles away where, we reasoned, Beever might behave himself, since the surroundings would be strange—I had a feeling that some of his actions might be due to a natural urge to defend his home territory from intruders. On that score I was wrong. At the Lindquists' the otter promptly crawled under a sofa and darted out to snap at any strange passing feet. Months later, in March, Ruth and Wally came again, and Beever was unpleasant again. Both of our visitors wore boots this time, and we decided to see what would develop. After a short time the otter lost his fear and approached the Lindquists often, sniffing at their boots and being almost friendly. Toward the end of an hour his patience at last wore thin, giving way to growls. When the intruders ignored those he grew calm again and finally wandered off into the bedroom for a nap.

At the end of March we visited the Linquists once more, and this time his behavior was no better, but the visit brought out two new facets of Beever's personality. Because he insisted on biting at Ruth's booted feet we had to confine him to their enclosed back porch, which connects with the kitchen via a sturdy Dutch door. Beever had always had trouble in standing upright—or at least he gave that impression. I used to try to make him sit up by holding a morsel of meat above his head, but I soon learned that I had to hold the meat out at arm's length, or Beever would climb up my leg and prop himself upright with one paw against it. Once I caught on to this tactic Beever began to use the kitchen cabinets for the same purpose, until I began holding the training sessions out in the middle of the floor. He would then rise reluctantly and, once up, seemed to have difficulty in maintaining the posture; if the meat was not given to him quickly he dropped back to the floor. Poor Beever, I thought.

At the Lindquists', every time I managed to slip through the door and close it before my otter could get through he stood bolt upright, quickly and easily, and held the pose unsupported for long minutes, peering at me as I leaned over the lower half of the door and chittering his annoyance. When we were home, of course, he reverted to his old exhausted act again.

Beever's second revelation at the Lindquists' was a fondness for avocado. I don't recall why I offered it to him, in view of his extraordinarily fussy eating habits, but when I held out a small slice he devoured it greedily.

Back in December our enforced solitude had begun to weigh heavily on me, to the point where, otter-be-damned, I was going to get away from home. Marion McCrane, a girl who had worked in the Bronx Zoo's Education Department and was now at the National Zoo in Washington, invited me to come and visit. Since I could not expect anyone to take care of the animals for me, they had to come along. Happily, the director of the National Zoo gave me permission to quarter the animals there, and Lear Grimmer, the Zoo's associate director, offered to let me stay at his home.

On a Thursday morning at eight-thirty I loaded the car, a new VW station wagon, for what was to be its maiden voyage. The old car, which I had taken in for servicing regularly, had in the fall just past jarred to an abrupt stop (fortunately in a town, at slow speed) because, as it turned out, the service shop had not checked the transmission lubricant. When, after the installation of a new transmission, I got home to find that the installer had seated a gasket improperly and the fluid was streaming out, I decided to sell the old buggy (after they made good on new repairs) and get a new one. I am, alas, committed to the VW as the only station wagon large enough for my animals. The new car was fully lined and much quieter, and had a divided front seat so that I could check on the animals in back without leaving the car.

The journey was a ghastly one. Beever chittered loudly for

over an hour before subsiding into sleep, and halfway to Washington it began to rain heavily. I suppose I have driven in every kind of weather and the conditions outside have never bothered me, but when the outside came inside I objected. The air intake on the VW wagon is located directly above the windshield, and the air is ducted through a box over the front seat, with a manually controlled outlet. I had the air shut off, but the driving rain found an uncaulked seam in the box and began to drip down onto the dashboard, short-circuiting the radio in no time at all. Far worse, the water continued downward, dripping squarely onto the accelerator pedal. Not that the pedal got very wet—as anyone who drives an automobile knows, the pedal of a moving car is protected from such things by the driver's right foot. When I pulled off onto the shoulder of the Turnpike to see what I could do about this soggy state of affairs Beever awakened and resumed his *a cappella* paean of annoyance. The upshot was that I had the option of keeping my foot under the drip and getting to Washington as soon as possible or sitting somewhere in southern New Jersey with a merely half-wet foot and a squawking otter. We resumed the trip.

The journey to Washington takes six hours by VW; I arrived with one very wet right foot. Beever, Pixie, and two small animals that I was taking to the Zoo as part of a trade. Several times, while Beever was awake, I had reached a hand back near his crate to reassure him. Each time he fell silent, as he reached out both of his handlike paws to clasp my fingers and pull them to him, to press them tightly against his nose.

At the Small Mammal House of the Zoo a cage and a half had been prepared for the otter. It was one of the several cages that are waterproof and heavily glassed, and can be used dry to house terrestrial species or filled with water to a depth of about three feet for aquatic ones. When filled, the cage can be used with the upper half of a duplex cage adjoining it, to provide a land surface, and this is how the cage had been prepared for Beever. Pixie's quarters were a holding cage in the service area.

Once in his temporary quarters, Beever chittered his unhappiness with earsplitting cries. From the rear service alley where I had put him into the cage, I moved quickly to the public space in front, as Beever, complaining loudly, followed my every move. I walked, slowly and very deliberately, past the barred front of the land area, past the pool, and Beever, rather than lose sight of me, stepped reluctantly into the water. Instantly he forgot me in the near-panic of his predicament. All his life he had known only the bathtub where, in no more than the ten inches of water it held, his paws could keep in contact with the bottom. And now he found himself in what was for him a bottomless abyss. Somehow he managed to turn about and scrabble wildly upon land again, terrified, despite his actual mastery of swimming. I reassured him, then left, with his protests reverberating through the halls of the huge building. Later that evening Marion and I returned to the building to find Beever resting quietly. Rather than have him begin chittering again we stood silently some distance from his cage and watched him for a while, then left for dinner at the Grimmers'.

Friday morning I followed Lear to the Zoo, where Marion and I went to look in on the otter. At a distance Beever showed no signs of recognition until I spoke, at which he burst into agitated activity, and when I approached his cage he began to chitter wildly. He tried to pull my extended hand, or at least a finger, through the bars to gnaw on it in his usual way, but I had to decline because the narrow spacing of the bars left me no room to "roll" with the otter's twisting pulls—the secret of avoiding a friendly laceration or two. The keeper in charge of the building, one of the best small-mammal men in the country, had succeeded in getting Beever to eat his day's ration of the beef which I had brought along (he had never before touched any meat tainted with a human scent other than mine) and had tied a dry towel to the bars for Beever to rub on. In addition Beever had mastered the "bottomless" tank overnight, and now pursued my hand as I moved it in complicated arabesques in front of the tank. That evening Marion and I dined in a French restaurant, where I ate my first—and last—snail. This has nothing to do with Beever's story, except that I thought very little about him all evening. Nor had I need to, for otters seem to be among the most psychologically resilient of animals.

Even more encouraging than Beever's lack of hostility toward the keeper (who had, after all, been feeding him) was his behavior toward Marion on the following day, as I readied him for the trip home. Marion met me at the Zoo with "an old blanket" she had offered to provide to keep Beever warm (she had obviously just bought it, but it was too late to argue). When the keeper and I had loaded Beever into the crate he had not growled at the man at all, which still surprised me. But when Marion came on the scene the otter, now in the VW, reached out through the crate and took her hand gently between his own, the first act of affection I had ever seen him lavish on another human. Pixie, in his own crate, was his usual surly self.

The return trip home was uneventful, though again Beever chittered for about an hour and thereafter fell silent, except for those times when the car slowed, stopped, or swerved sharply. When we arrived home late in the evening Beever seemed weak and limp, and during the night I heard the plaintive quavering cry that signals distress. He was asleep when he uttered the cries, and I suppose that he was reliving in his dreams the more unhappy moments of his solitude in Washington. That he had not been in real distress after our return home was indicated by his hearty appetite, which continued in the morning. During the day he seemed more sensitive to my touch than normally, and walked stiffly, probably as a result of increased activity that first night in the strange cage, and the greater than usual amount of swimming he did subsequently. His first night's agitation was attested to by his blunted claws, worn down as he tried to dig his way out of the concrete cage. By the afternoon of our first day home, though, he was completely back to normal.

Luke and Dotty Wisbeski, who are among my closest friends if the degree to which I have imposed upon them is any measure, came into my life and Beever's not long after the cub's arrival. Since my active involvement with, and commitment to, otters, I have come to know a greater number of otter people than I had ever suspected could exist, and in many cases what began as an unabashed bit of brain-picking on my part has grown into friendship. A few of these otter people have reached the point where they could no longer keep their animals, and the Zoo's otter population has grown a little as a result, to the point where at one time there was an otter on semi-exhibit in one moated yard of the Great Apes House. In this case the yard was otherwise unused, as its old occupant then shared a larger one with another gorilla. The otter had been put there because, just prior to her arrival, she had come in contact with a dog suffering from canine distemper (another disease to which otters are susceptible), and every other cage that had water available was too close to the other otters for comfort. The otter was unfortunate enough to arrive at a time when even the quarantine section in the Animal Hospital was occupied by another otter. As a result, I was cruelly exposed for a long time to the director's not overly flattering allusions to my lutraphilia.

The Wisbeskis' Okee, because he was about a month older than Beever, was at first a combined source of scientifically significant growth data and handy barometer to me of what to expect in Beever's life. Although I came to feel a great personal concern for him, to me Okee was always a wild animal to whom I was unable to give my full trust. I do not mean in any way to imply a fault in Okee; rather, the otters that came to share my board and, I am ashamed to admit, my bed have beguiled me into according to them a trust that is exceptional for me.

I have never been accused of being dapper, but on the evening of the Wisbeskis' visit I decided that, after all, they had an otter and I might as well forgo staying in the suit I wore at the Zoo and dress in my coping-with-Beever clothes, including the ill-used old khaki trousers whose one threadbare knee Beever had rent and then opened farther. The old engineer boots I needed because of the otter's penchant for chewing on feet, which was as painful as it was playful. I was indeed a sorry sight, particularly in view of the appearance of my guests, who were dressed like a civilized lady and gentleman. Beever greeted them with a growl, an endless series of growls actually, interspersed with "Hah's." Dotty's flouncy skirt didn't help matters, but even when she seated herself on the sofa my otter was unquiet, and secreted himself under one piece of furniture or another during most of the evening. Several times from under the sofa he made short rushes at unwelcome feet but they were bluffs that fell short of their mark. Although Okee was outside in their car I was chary of a meeting between the two otters and we decided to postpone the introduction. For one reason or another the otters did not meet until March.

Luke and Dotty met a more civil but still somewhat aloof Beever when they arrived on their next visit. He growled only once, spent some time sniffing at their feet, and relaxed enough in their presence to play with me. Then Okee was brought in.

By this time Beever had attained nearly his full growth; he spanned, as nearly as a conscious otter can be measured, about forty inches from nose to tail-tip, and weighed about fifteen pounds, almost precisely what an otter from northern Colombia should weigh and measure according to the meager information available. Okee dwarfed him. The Wisbeskis' otter then weighed over twenty-three pounds and was, by my estimate, about forty-eight inches long. (Before the illness that preceded his death early in 1967 Okee measured fifty-eight inches and weighed forty-five pounds without being pudgy.) From the beginning Okee's feet were larger than Beever's, and he seemed merely to have grown into them. The two otters were collected from the same vicinity as nearly as I can ascertain, and apart from size showed no other significant differences. Unfortunately there are so few museum specimens of otters from South America that the range of variation has never been determined, and this is one of the problems that I have been attempting to investigate.

At first glance all *Lutra* otters look alike, apart from the shapes of their nose patches. Still, although they were not immediately evident to me, I have begun to notice other more subtle differences. In the Colombian otters of the Rio Magdalena drainage, for example, the change from the dark-brown color of the otters' upper parts to the pale grayishness of the undersides does not happen abruptly on the head and neck as it does in North American otters or those from the Amazon drainage. There is almost imperceptible gradation. Further unlike the North American ones, otters from the northern reaches of

South America do not have uniformly colored undersides, but frequently bear orangy splotches on the neck, chest, or belly—sometimes on all of these areas. There is no uniformity of arrangement from one individual to the next, and if one could see the undersides of wild-living otters in South America he could doubtless distinguish every otter he saw from all others. Beever had the usual white upper lip and chin (the flesh of the lips is pink in South American otters, darkly pigmented in those from North America). On his chest he bore a saffron heart-shaped

blotch that became paler as he grew; between his hind legs was a longitudinal, irregularly-edged streak followed by a transverse series of two dots and a dash, all in the same color. (Okee had only a small, roughly triangular chest patch and the long belly streak. Goop had had his own personal markings and Mimsy, who would come along much later, had hers, too.)

For maximum control of the situation Okee was brought into the house on a leash; Beever had been put into his travel cage. The meeting of the otters was deafening, with a continuous exchange of chittering as Beever pawed at Okee through the cage. When, after a few minutes, neither otter had displayed the least sign of hostility we reversed the otters, with Okee inside the cage, and again all went well. I detected some slight edginess in both animals, but the predominant feeling was amiability. Luke then took Okee out into porch while I put a harness and leash on Beever, and again we brought our charges together. Again they behaved themselves, and at length we unleashed them. At first Beever hid briefly under the phonograph console, but soon he was out and the otters began to play in the same

way Beever and Goop had played with the fennec, pawing and nipping and lolling on their backs. Most interesting to me was the revelation that Beever had, in some ways at least, treated Pixie as he did another otter. Pixie, incidentally, did not absent himself totally from the proceedings; several times he scuttled up behind Okee, first to sniff at his tail, then to nip playfully at it.

In April, Mom and my Aunt Alix initiated a practice of more or less regular visits by day. Their original intent was to hang new curtains, but they expanded from this task to a partial but female-thorough housecleaning operation, which has fortunately continued. On that first day I stayed home. In recent days Beever had learned to force the flimsy latch that kept him confined by day, and while I slept, to "his" half of the house, and I replaced the old latch with a barrel bolt while the women worked. Beever resented his exile and chittered frenziedly much of the time. Not that he really wanted to be let out, for the bustle of feet and mops and brooms he saw disquieted him further. I tried to soothe him by running water in the tub, but for the first time in his life water was not what he wanted. Every time I walked away from the tub he followed at my heels. At length I was forced to heave him away from the study door and bolt it quickly.

That evening, when we were alone again, Beever found that his world had changed. In his time my efforts at cleaning floors had been sporadic and limited to spot-cleaning and general sweeping. Now he found himself faced (outside of "his" part of the house, which had been left alone this time) with floors that smelled of cleaning materials and, perhaps more important to him, floors which lacked the comfortable scent of his own comings and goings. He poked around, particularly in the corners where possibly the detergent had not been so effective, but in the main he acted bewildered and a trifle edgy. At first he refused to eat from his dish in the kitchen until it occurred to him to snatch up a mouthful and carry it to the study to eat. When I moved the dish from the spotless kitchen floor to the study he finished its contents without delay.

6   The Rise and Fall of the Otter-proof Bed

       Young animals, in my experience, will continue to nurse for as long as their mothers permit, even long after they are capable of digesting solid food. In nature the point of complete weaning seems to be left largely up to the forbearance of the female, but it seems equally true that the youngster's first interest in solid food comes some time before it is really capable of subsisting without milk. Sometimes an orphan manages to survive a premature weaning, but it does so with difficulty. Two schools of thought exist concerning the weaning of animals reared by hand. One favors as early a weaning as possible, at or near the animal's first willingness to tackle solid food. The other, which I follow, holds to continuing milk for a longer period, tapering off very gradually. Otters in particular appear to require a far greater liquid intake than other mammals of comparable size, and milk is an excellent source. I know of at least one prematurely weaned otter that I watched die of dehydration in the hands of a person who found the frequent sessions with a bottle tiresome. I determined not to let Beever suffer the same fate.

Beever already had a taste for meat when he arrived, but he took his Esbilac (a simulated bitch's milk formula) readily after the inevitable initial triumph of human will power over the cub's reluctance to accept an un-otterlike nipple. I had abandoned all thought of using a human baby-bottle when I had Goop (the usual doll's-bottle nipple is too small and too short for even a baby otter's cavernous mouth). At that time I found that a rubber ear-syringe worked well, once the cub stopped struggling against its hard narrow tip. It had the advantage of being firm enough to pry apart clamped, unwilling jaws, and the rubber bulb allowed me to express milk at a controlled rate. Beever, like Goop, resisted the counterfeit teat mightily, but at length the taste of the Esbilac overrode his aversion to its method of delivery. For the rest of his life after weaning I allowed him an occasional treat of Esbilac, and at the sight of the ear-syringe he would all but climb my legs to reach it. The reason for allowing Beever his occasional milk was a practical one—during his sporadic enteric difficulties I could introduce oral medication mixed with Esbilac via the syringe, and he always took it without a struggle. I might add parenthetically here that one cannot wean an otter as one does a puppy or kitten with solids and milk in a bowl, since otter cubs will bathe in anything they find in a bowl. One does it like a mother otter, by offering adult foods while still giving milk separately.

One trait common to all of the cubs I have seen has been their finickiness in the matter of food. Some ate beef but not horsemeat, others vice versa. None would touch fish; in spite of the fact that fish form a large part of the diet of most species of otter the taste seems to be an acquired one, born of necessity.

But the one thing every otter cub I have seen, without exception, will pounce upon and devour greedily is chicken, both raw and cooked.

Chicken was all right for a starter, but it is an inconvenient diet from the human viewpoint; for one thing chickens take up too much room in the refrigerator. All the while continuing Esbilac feedings, I began to experiment with diets. Beever ate horsemeat, even with dog-meal mixed in, but horsemeat was almost impossible to obtain. The Zoo receives regular shipments of fresh horsemeat at about half the cost of comparably fresh meat available to me elsewhere if I wanted to make frequent long trips to buy it. But the Zoo is so large that the accounting problems involved in my purchasing Zoo meat would be very involved, so I abandoned any thought of using Zoo meat and settled at last for beef chuck, which is not inexpensive. I made up my own mixture with vitamins and bone meal, cereal and Esbilac, but the otter cared little for it, and for a while I put Beever on a diet of chunks of beef chuck, which he relished. One morning I noticed him eating something in the empty bathtub, a decaying bit of meat. This was before he and Pixie met; the diarrhea that followed made it clear that Pixie's caches would need to be monitored. The sulfadimethoxine pill prescribed for him had little effect, and Dr. Wolf then gave me a liquid neomycin product, Biosol M, which, administered in Esbilac at a rate of one drop per three pounds of body weight, saw Beever through this and all subsequent bouts of bacterial enteritis.

Several times, after violent play on a full stomach, Beever vomited his partly digested meal but like many animals immediately reingested most of it. This kind of vomiting was a very different thing from the kind that produced the watery, foul-smelling liquid by obviously painful retching, when the otter

G

was plagued by his occasional bacterial invasions. Another food additive that helped control Beever's enteric bacteria was one I discovered in an article in a veterinary journal. Cultures of *Lactobacillus acidophilus* and *L. bulgaricus,* the bacteria that produce buttermilk and yogurt, when introduced into the digestive tract proliferate into a nontoxic flora that is inimical to the bacteria of putrefaction which cause enteritis. When introduced with milk, *Lactobacillus* multiplies rapidly. In the meantime a letter from Emil Liers, who has reared scores of North American otters, disclosed that he regularly added a similar culture to his otter food. My first attempts at getting Beever to eat yogurt, the most convenient form of *Lactobacillus* I knew of, fell short of success. He did take a little if I mixed it well with ground meat, but the quantity of bacteria could not be great. Luckily the drugstore had packets of dehydrated *Lactobacillus,* apparently tasteless, and Beever took this form in Esbilac without an argument. I used the cultures sparingly with Beever only when he was ill, but have since made it a regular ingredient of my otter meat mixture.

After a particularly violent siege of enteritis in mid-April, one which seemed not to be responding to the oral medication, I called Dotty Wisbeski, who had just brought Okee through a similarly virulent attack, and she gave me the list of medications used with success by her veterinarian. Because a car trip seemed likely to aggravate my otter's distress I drove alone to Dr. Wolf's, and he gave me a syringe and the medicines (neomycin and polymixin B, to control the enterotoxic bacteria, and a cortisone-type drug to pick up the otter's appetite). Treating Beever, that is, sticking a hypodermic needle into him single-handed, was out of the question, so I called Ruth Lindquist, who is a registered nurse. I found that I could control Beever's head by grasping him on both sides of it, just below the ears, and pulling out a fistful of loose skin; in this hold he couldn't get his teeth into either of us (I think), but his body from the head back was his own to flail about at will, and Ruth couldn't get near him with the needle. In a flash of inspiration I placed the otter in his traveling crate and pulled his ample tail out through the widely-spaced bars, bracing my foot against the crate to hold it steady. Ruth administered both shots cleanly and easily about five inches from the base of the tail, and after a quick squawk Beever behaved as if nothing had happened. That was at a quarter after one in the afternoon. When Beever seemed to be improving I left to have dinner with my parents in Jersey City, and when I came home a little before midnight Beever was a ball of fire. His play was vigorous beyond belief, his bites more painful than usual, and his appetite enormous.

During my visit to Dr. Wolf he had given me a canned dog-cat food available only through veterinarians. Although Beever's previous reaction to canned foods had been negative I tried some on the chance that the cortisone-heightened appetite might induce him to eat it. On the night of his injections the otter disdained the new food but the next day he wolfed it down as eagerly as he did the beef, offered at the same time. Thereafter Beever's diet consisted largely of the canned food (which had a high caloric content) with occasional meat, a regimen that could facilitate travel, since we would no longer have to carry, and refrigerate, fresh meat. Beever seemed satisfied with the menu and as far as I could tell remained just as healthy as he had been when eating fresh meat exclusively.

From time to time I offered new kinds of food to Beever, most of which didn't appeal to him. He would on occasion eat such foods as cod, unflavored yogurt, and cream cheese with chives, as well as avocado slices, but I never made any of these a regular part of his diet. While he normally took his regular foods by mouth from the bowl, his response to any new item was characteristic. After an initial confident approach to the dish he would stop short, then retreat a step or two from the unfamiliar scent. Next he would approach the dish with extreme caution, stretching as far forward as he could from the shoulders, leaving his forepaws planted solidly, ready to pull back instantly. Now he would sniff cautiously, then extend a paw into the dish to rake out some of its contents. When he was safely back from the dish, Beever's olfactory investigation of the sample would lead him either to nibble tentatively or turn up his nose at the food. This use of his forepaws to take food was one of the few instances where he forsook the use of his mouth, but it bears a similarity to the manipulation that is so commonly practiced by the African and Asiatic clawless otters (*Aonyx*), which the Germans more aptly call *Fingerotters*.

Although there seemed to be no sensible reason for including fish in the otter's menu, but because free-living otters do consume fish in quantity, I decided to try Beever with a butterfish I brought home from the Zoo. At first he ignored it, until I dropped the fish into the bathtub as the otter was playing. As far as I could tell he treated it then as just another toy, wrestling with it, pawing at it, and eventually taking it in his mouth—this he would have done with any object of the same size. At last, as I had expected, his play led him to bite harder and he got a taste of the fish, which by now was well thawed. Later he hauled himself out of the tub with the fish in his mouth, growling the while. He poked about the bathroom aimlessly, seemingly in search of a place to eat the fish, then disappeared into the bedroom where he ate his booty.

Beever's growling over food was an interesting phenomenon. Initially, upon arrival Beever and Goop (and later Mimsy) stood over their food and growled as they ate; I believed at the time that the growls were directed toward me specifically, but I'm not so sure any more. The idea of being threatened held little appeal, so I set out to rectify the situation with Goop. Luckily my technique worked and has been successful with the other cubs as well. Instead of feeding the cubs their meat in a dish I made a point of offering it piece by piece from my hand. Naturally each cub's first response was a cautious, stretching approach, followed by a snatching at the meat and retreating to consume it. Rapidly each gained confidence, though, and within the first day hand-feeding was the accepted procedure. Apparently the otters learned that the hand that fed them was no enemy; soon I could remove the meat from their mouths with impunity, and when we returned to dish-feeding I could pluck out the food from the dish even while the otter's muzzle was there. Beever was particularly good in this respect, and let even the fennec steal food from under his nose. But all this good behavior involved soft, ground meat or small cubes that were bite-sized. On the few occasions when I gave him meat in large chunks about six inches long, or a whole butterfish, his attitude changed and he would carry his meal off, usually to the bedroom, growling continuously. What made the growls odd was that they were not directed at me or at Pixie, who was never nearby, but they seemed merely to be directed "to whom it may concern." As a zoologist I should have called the otter's bluff when he growled that way, but I was more strongly disposed to respect his claim, in this case not because of a fear of being bitten but just because he was a friend, and one should, occasionally at least, respect a friend's desire for privacy.

Bill Conway, the Bronx Zoo's director, delighted in introducing me to people as "Joe Davis—he sleeps with an otter." It's all very amusing, Lord knows, and I'd enjoy it too if he were talking about someone else. The trouble is, I'm not particularly keen on sharing my bed with an otter. I am firmly committed to the belief that a wild animal is trustworthy only to the extent that one is aware of its presence. I have never believed in so much as momentarily relaxing my vigilance in the presence of any wild animal that is not safely caged, much less sleeping in its presence, and I don't approve of it now. However, I was stuck with a situation I had little practical control over.

Goop was the first otter to take to my bed. I slept in those days on a perfectly normal, everyday bed—a four-inch-thick urethane foam mattress on a box spring resting on a metal Harvard frame. Despite the firmness of the foam mattress, the bed was still too soft for my liking, and I had inserted a 3/4-inch plywood sheet between the mattress and the box spring. The top of the mattress, incidentally, measured about nineteen inches from the floor. At first I excluded Goop from the bedroom by pulling the double doors closed, but in time he learned to open them and eventually to climb on the bed in my absence. Before retiring I barricaded the doors with a concrete block (no Otter Person should be without concrete blocks in his home— they come in handy for so many things), but once he knew about the bed he chittered outside the door endlessly. I remained resolute until Goop's last illness, when I relented to bolster his spirits.

Life with Beever began in much the same spirit of human supremacy. I had abandoned all thought of locking him out of the bedroom early in our association because, while Goop had not lived more than a few weeks, Beever's happy longevity accumulated weeks of nocturnal chitterings and I began to grow haggard from lack of sleep. For a while things went well. Beever contented himself with sleeping under the dresser or the bed, and if occasionally he chittered for attention I could drop my hand down to the floor to satisfy him with a touch. My sleeping habits present me with both a blessing and a curse; the curse involves my inability to fall asleep under even the slightest disruptive influence, and an otter's piercing protest is far from slight. The blessing is that, once asleep, I could be transported via pogo stick to the rim of an erupting volcano without disturbing in the least the seven-hour torpor my body and mind demand each night. Having crossed the brink of unconsciousness I slumber deeply, come hell, high water, or lonely otter.

By the time he had been with me two months Beever mastered the difficult climb to the bed, partly because of his increase in size and partly because he had learned to use his claws for purchase—and without question it had also come within his knowledge that the bed was a desirable place. An otter's claws arise from the upper surface of the digits. Short and stout, they point slightly upward. The otter manipulates small objects without recourse to his claws, and if he takes your finger in this fashion the touch is indescribably delicate. But when the otter flexes his fingers, his claws are brought into a usable position. With them he can climb a tree or attempt to climb your leg. Worst of all, when I leaned forward on the sofa to type (inevitably my sweatshirt rode upward in back) Beever would sprawl out next to me and scrabble rapidly on my exposed skin as though he were trying to dig a hole. A deep one. He was not, of course, really trying to dig, but merely indulging in a form of play the significance of which was presumably more clear to him than to me. When scratching at a flea an otter holds his toes in the same partially flexed position, to allow the claws to do their work.

Beever used his claws to dig into the box spring when climbing into bed; he also used them to tear open the ticking under the spring and pull out quantities of stuffing, but what went on under the bed concerned me less than what happened topside. It reminded me of the hammock that one of Marion's skunks had made by tearing the ticking under her box spring, and if she could be proud of a thing like that I could at least tolerate something in the same category.

The daytime visits to my bed were no secret; the pillow on the floor, an occasional set of fecal footprints, or the telephone off its cradle were dead giveaways. The telephone and the pillow were minor irritations, but the footprints were, so to speak, the handwriting on the wall. I otterproofed the bed. This I did by pulling the plywood bedboard out until it protruded about eight inches past the mattress and box spring. Beever could reach the board easily enough with his forepaws, but the overhang was enough to keep him from getting purchase on the spring with his hind feet, and after dangling in futility for a while he would abandon his attempts to climb. Unfortunately the board was cut for a bed of standard length, and my new bed was an extra-long one; in no time at all Beever discovered the eight inches toward the foot where there was no protecting board. I hunted up a scrap of plywood from the cellar and extended the overhang, a tactic that stopped him for a few more days. ·

The room I adopted for a bedroom is a narrow one and the bed lay along one of the short walls; with a cabinet-type headboard the bed took up almost the entire width, with about six inches to spare at the foot. In no time at all Beever learned to shinny up in the space between the foot of the bed and the wall, and again I added pieces of plywood for a barrier, until at last I felt as though I were bedded down on a lumberyard. Still the otter found ways to reach his objective, and I would awaken in the morning to feel soft bristles in my face and hear the innocent, amiable chuckle of the beast who had overcome all obstacles to be with me. Mornings were not too bad, but Beever's nocturnal visits I did not welcome.

At first Beever confined his visits to the time I awoke, although it is possible that he may have arrived at any time after I fell asleep. With time, though, his ascents came earlier, during that precarious interlude between consciousness and slumber when my compassion was more torpid than my temper. Some subconscious feeling of guilt, I suppose, had caused me to omit the incidents of this period from my notes; still, I remember what happened. One particularly insomniac night when Beever was determined to climb into bed with me—how he surmounted my barriers I no longer remember, but suddenly there he was, lurching over me. I grasped him by the scruff of his neck and deposited him with a rude thump on the floor. In the next instant he was back, and I repeated the eviction. To make the story short, Beever was not to be dissuaded and little by little my response grew less and less gentle, until I found myself hurling him across the room (or at least it seemed that way). Thump! Beever would hit the floor some few feet from the bed and skitter off a little farther; then I'd hear the flat-footed patter of his little feet approaching the bed at a dead run and once again he was with me. At last a time came when the thump was followed by silence. As I lay in the lightless room, listening and hearing nothing, I became suddenly aware of what I had been doing. Suddenly despising myself in the realization of my actions I reached for the light switch, but even before I could illuminate the room the sound of otter feet reached my ears. By the time I had put the light on Beever was back in bed.

I allowed him to stay awhile after my scare, but after a few minutes of sharing my bed with a very wide-awake otter it was obvious that I would be in no condition to get up in the morning. This time I deposited Beever outside the bedroom and barricaded the door with a concrete block. I should have known better than to exile the cub to a room he was not accustomed to sleeping in, but then I wasn't totally awake at the time. Beever stationed himself outside the door and chittered away at the top of his lungs. At length, in a hour so desolate that I don't recall whether I acted to soothe him or myself, I opened the door and fell back onto the bed into a deep sleep, with Beever beside me.

It is to Beever's credit that he learned so quickly that the bed was a place for sleeping and not playing. It would be as inaccurate to say that Beever slept *on* my bed as to say *in* it; properly speaking, he slept *throughout* the bed, most often next to my pillow, but also at my feet or my side, between the sheets or under the lower one, or simply between the top sheet and blanket. My own sleeping habits underwent a change, too. I had taken by this time to wearing ski pajamas, and now I had to learn to sleep on my back. I awoke one morning lying on my stomach, with an odd sensation I couldn't quite define, and when I tried to roll over on my side I realized that I was sharing the seat of my pants with a sleeping otter, a condition which must be matched in unpleasantness only by that of a baby in an unchanged diaper. When I reached down to extricate him the cub crawled downward along my leg, where the ankle cuff would prevent an exit. Somehow I succeeded in regaining sole occupancy of the pajamas and clouted Beever a good one. The future looked dismal.

So it was that I set about to build a truly otter-proof bed. The main consideration was that it be high enough from the floor to prevent climbing, so I bought five 30-inch lengths of iron pipe, and with my father's help threaded them to take flanges. These were the legs of the new bed. At a lumberyard I had a sheet of 3/4-inch plywood cut to form the mattress support, and I made it long enough so that, with the headboard cabinet in place, the bed was firmly wedged between the walls of the little room. Assembling the new bed was easier than I had anticipated and, finally, to fancy it up a bit I installed a bar of walnut along the outer edge to serve both as decoration and to keep the old mattress from sliding off (the box spring was discarded).

The new bed was comfortable, even if it did rest at table height. And with the air conditioner that I bought shortly after the bed was built, the remainder of the summer now promised to be fine.

My brother Pete installed it one Saturday, in what we decided was a sensible place, under the window other than the one my bed abutted. This location was best from a construction standpoint, and it was a good two feet away from the bed. With the clarity of hindsight, it became as obvious to me as to Beever that it was *only* two feet from the bed. Within weeks he learned to scramble up the grilled face of the machine, inch along the window sill, and with a small leap land on the new bed. When faced with this sort of determination in an animal, one must be firm. One must make up his mind at the outset that he is going to give up whatever the cost. And so I did. After all, I told myself, the damn otter was behaving himself lately. Then I pulled a chair close to the bed to make the precarious climb up the air conditioner unnecessary. Remarkably, Beever did behave himself, at least while I was in the bed.

Daytimes saw the same old depredations, plus a new one or two. Most often the telephone lay off the cradle, uttering the small, tinny, banshee-wail that the telephone company employs to remind subscribers, if not otters, that something is amiss. One evening when I slid into bed something crinkled under me—

Beever had found one of the papers the laundry slips into pressed shirts and pulled it under the sheet. Another night it was a flashlight. For a long time the cabinet in the headboard was safe; then Beever discovered that he could slide the doors open, and I found myself unmaking the bed in the middle of the night, retrieving the contents of a box of tissues that had been secreted under the blanket, between the sheets, and under the mattress. Thereafter the cabinet was Beever's, and he often slept within it.

Obviously a way had to be found to keep Beever out of bed in the daytime. Again those old stand-bys, plywood and a concrete block, came to the rescue. A sheet of plywood wide enough to provide an overhang, set atop the air conditioner and weighted with a concrete block, kept the otter away as long as I remembered to push the chair under the bed before leaving in the morning, which I usually did.

Only twice did Beever cause any real trouble at night. Once he pulled down the phone, which had been in its accustomed place atop the radio on the headboard. I had not yet achieved nirvana, and the crash brought up the beast in me. I began to cuff him about soundly, which attack he accepted without retaliation, until the air became suddenly redolent of musk. Beever must have been truly frightened, because he never excreted the stuff except under severe stress—unlike Okee, whose musking point was extremely low. At any rate, when I switched on the light I found a small, muddy-brown stain on the sheet. Fortunately otter musk, unlike that of the skunks, has little staying power, and by morning the odor had dissipated.

Several months later, at half past three of an April morning, I was awakened by a restless, noisy otter, scratching at me, something he had never done before in bed. Foolishly I didn't investigate sufficiently (perhaps foolishly is the wrong word—I wasn't sufficiently awake to be either foolish or wise). Be that as it may, I reacted as usual by cuffing him, severely enough to elicit a suffocating quantity of musk. By the time I thought to make a light it was too late; there at the foot of the bed was a large (but, happily, firm) stool. Only then did I notice that the chair was improperly placed. Beever could not leave the bed and his frenzy had been the very natural result of the urgent command of his bowels pitted against his frustrated attempts to leave the bed. I am ashamed to admit that in those desperate few moments when Beever had risen above his animal nature, seeking help from me, I had reacted in less than human fashion.

Telephones were a source of endless interest to Beever. Like Pixie, he often pulled out the removable wall jacks, but I took the view that this was preferable to having the animals work on connections meant to be permanent. Outside of this, and the matter of knocking the handset from its cradle, Beever did not really get involved with the phone until he had been with me nearly a year.

On an early spring Saturday, I awakened at half past five to find the otter chewing on my eyeglasses, which had been reposing in the headboard cabinet. Until this time Beever had not opened the sliding door in my presence—but he had been a demon ever since the cortisone injections he received when he was ill. From the glasses my gaze rose upward to the telephone, whose handset had been totally but not too neatly severed from the base. From each mangled end of the cord there protruded four colored wires, one red, one black, and two white ones. These indignities and the earliness of the hour caused me to render a terrible judgment upon this innocent fiend, after which I drew up the covers and sought to resume my interrupted sleep. In a few minutes I felt him climb past my feet, thump down on the chair, and patter off into the distance. A loud bang brought me bounding out of bed in a trice; first I discovered that I had forgotten to close the doors to the living room, and then, in the kitchen, there was Beever halfway into the broiler section of the stove. That did it! I locked him unceremoniously into his carrying case and returned to bed, to

awaken again in a normal fashion many hours later. The telephone man arrived and replaced the cord without comment. Four days later I left the unplugged telephone on the porch, after calling for repairs again, and the man installed another new cord. Shortly afterward I conceded defeat and had wall telephones installed.

Early in May I traveled to Maryland, where I had agreed to

look over a small municipal zoo and give some advice on expanding the facilities. In addition I was to investigate a stand of cypress with a view to obtaining a number of trees for our own Zoo's Aquatic Bird House, then under construction. While I was in the area I decided I could also nip over to the National Zoo. Luke and Dotty had long before offered to board Beever for me, but my usual preoccupation with everything from Beever to the Zoo put me in the ghastly position of giving my friends less than two days' notice of the trip. The Wisbeskis, characteristically, agreed without hesitation, in spite of a prior commitment to be in Ocean City. Their solution was direct and simple—they would take Beever with them. On the evening of 6 May, after work, I loaded Beever into the car, stopped off at the vet's for a case of canned food, and set off for South Bound Brook. At the Wisbeskis' Beever tried vainly at first to remain in character, hiding under the sofa and growling, emerging only to follow my retreating footsteps into another room. Luke, on the other hand, was determined to crack the otter's defensive shell and, true to his own character, wasted little time in the attempt. There have been few times during my association with otters when I have experienced the slow-motion unfolding of an action in minute detail as if I were a detached observer at a movie; I was about to witness the first one. It began as I saw Luke reach for Beever, who was in the middle of the Wisbeski living room, following me. As Luke bent over, and his intention of touching Beever dawned on me, so also there began to grow a feeling of impending disaster. Luke had both massive hands on the otter, lifted him—it seemed with the slow grace of an underwater ballet—and clutched him to his chest. Beever's jaws were inches from Luke's throat. He began to struggle.

After the tense moments that passed so slowly the action slipped back to normal speed. Beever was still struggling, but not any more violently than he did when I held him. I had fully expected Beever to "defend" himself, to twist back and slash Luke's hands, or worse, to attack his vulnerable throat. He did neither, and when Luke set him down on the floor again Beever had made a friend. But Dotty's ballooning skirt was too much for him in spite of his new outlook on people, and Beever continued to treat her with reserve until she began wearing slacks. I left for Maryland on the following day and met Luke and Dotty in Ocean City, New Jersey, on the return trip as we had planned, on the afternoon of the tenth.

Although my first summers were all passed at the seashore I have never been very enthusiastic about it, and in later years I can recall only one visit to the ocean on a day that was not blustery. The day of my arrival at Ocean City was one of the usual ones, cold, gray, and windy, but Dotty insisted that we take the otters for a walk along the beach. Women, like otters, must be given in to immediately if one is to have any peace at all, so I acceded after a brief but broad show of reluctance. Okee, it was obvious, enjoyed the romp, as did Trouper, the Wisbeskis' dog. Beever did deign to dip his belly in the water, but no more, and after an endless trek during which the wind began to knife through both my heavy sweater and sweatshirt and my ears began to ache, Beever and I came simultaneously to the conclusion that we had had enough. He simply retracted his short legs and refused to move farther; I seized upon this and suggested that we return. Dotty gave in graciously, but another problem arose; Beever, who would not take another step forward, would not take another step, period. With some urging and tugging at the leash I could get him to take a few steps, but each brief sally ended in a squat. He was exhausted.

Only one alternative remained, and rather than try to carry a

Mimsy

Sam

squirming otter in my arms I tucked him under my sweater. (The sweatshirt protected me from most of the sand that clung to his belly and only a little worked its way into my underpants.) Now Beever was faced with two equally unpleasant choices. He was not accustomed to being imprisoned under my clothing and he wanted out; since I had by this time tucked the sweater into my trousers, the only egress was through the tight neck of the thing, and, because my own neck already occupied most of the opening, he could emerge only as far as his collarbone, and protrude one forepaw, which reached to my larynx. Thus exposed he rode a while, his face in mine, paw pressed firmly against my Adam's apple, chittering. When he had stood the wind as long as he could he would duck back into the sweater and subside for a while until he regained strength of spirit enough to repeat the process. Thus we retraced our steps, Beever being a very noisy jack-in-the-box all the way. Luke seemed to be enduring the weather well, and Okee, Trouper, and Dotty were plainly returning only to be accommodating.

On the ride from Ocean City the Volkswagen broke down. On my last visit to the service department a mechanic had, I discovered, failed to tighten a connection on the heater after working on it, and the heater bracket had fallen, pressing a very hot wire against the cables that connect the distributor to the spark plugs. The hot wire had neatly burned through three of the four cables. Luke, who was following behind in his car, pulled up to help, but the seemingly simple solution to the severed cables evaporated shortly. Obviously, we had to splice the cut wires together. When we shaved off the thick plastic insulation, though, there was no wire. Thinking we had cut too deeply, we tried again, with the same result. At last I began to suspect that despite the absence of a wire in the cable *something*

H

had to be a conductor, so we inserted a short length of copper wire that Luke had in his car into the center of each cable, and the VW started as if nothing had been amiss. Later I was told by the VW people that, indeed, there was no wire in the cable, which used a conductive plastic instead. At any rate, we were on our way again and arrived home with no further trouble.

7   A Study in Purple

Beever had an uncanny way of knowing when I arrived home in the evenings. At first I assumed that he used the radio as his clue, because the first thing I did upon arriving was to turn it on. Often I let the otter out of his confinement as soon as I came home (I would then usually find him asleep), but there were days when I was so tired that I needed a brief time of stretching out on the sofa before I could face the inevitable rough-and-tumble greeting that Beever reserved for me. To forestall what I thought was his auditory clue I began to leave the bedroom radio on all day, and to play the living room radio softly when I wanted solitude; it didn't work, and the otter would be at the door chittering less than a quarter of an hour after my return. Somewhat later I discovered what was giving me away. After tending to the radio, I realized, I always turned up the thermostat setting and the temperature rise gave away my secret. The way in which this revelation came to me was not due to my superior powers of ratiocination but to a change in the weather; two warm days in May were responsible.

On the fourteenth it was warm enough to leave the house without activating the furnace, and I left the thermostat alone when I got home. As it happened I was dead tired, so I switched the radio on and stretched out on the sofa, where I all but fell asleep. About an hour and a half later, at eight o'clock, it dawned on me that Beever was unusually silent (I have a keen, perceptive mind) and I unlatched the study door. As I did so Beever's chittering "rally" call issued from the bedroom. I called to him but the chittering continued, a sign that he either would not or could not come to me. I found him stranded on the bed. Evidently he had climbed to it via the air conditioner, a new accomplishment at that time, only to find the descent too steep to navigate. Thus trapped, Beever had found himself with an abundance of time at his disposal. As Gavin Maxwell has so aptly put it, "otters are extremely bad at doing nothing," and Beever had indeed not twiddled his figurative thumbs whiling away the time until rescue. The electric alarm clock was on its side and the radio askew. The headboard cabinet doors gaped open and turquoise tissues were scattered over the blanket. My pajamas were tucked in a lump under the bottom sheet. The sheet bore a smallish frayed hole that he had scratched through and the pillow lay on the floor. When later I changed the sheets there were more tissues under them, and under the mattress as well.

A cardinal rule in animal training is that punishment must be meted out at the time of the infraction or it will serve no purpose, so I merely moved the chair close to the bed and let Beever climb down. Later that evening after a session in the tub my keen mind warned me a second or two too late that I had better pull the chair away from the bed again, and when I arrived on the scene I found a wet otter languorously scrootching from side to side on the sheets. This time, since I had discovered the culprit in the midst of a foul deed, I laced into him with a heavy hand and a clear conscience, and he responded by acting properly contrite and guilty.

22 May produced Beever's greatest triumph. It was his finest hour, if one can speak with pride of an atrocity. I remember it, with chromatic license, as the Purple Letter Day.

Gordon Cooper, the astronaut, spent part of the day in a triumphal ticker-tape parade in Manhattan, surrounded by bits of paper floating down through the air; for me it was an uneventful but exhausting Wednesday at the Park, and when I arrived home about six-thirty I sprawled out on the sofa without even bothering to turn the radio on. Eight o'clock seems to be a significant hour, because at that time I began to notice Beever's silence again. It was then that the role of the thermostat in the otter's activity cycle was confirmed, for the day was warm and I hadn't tampered with its setting. There had, of course, been other warm days in the interim, but on those days I had arrived chipper enough to turn Beever loose at once, rousting him out of his den under the bed.

At eight I reluctantly got up and opened the door. Again I found Beever in my bed, in his favorite forbidden place under the bottom sheet. I had neglected to reset the plywood and cement block. That explained *that,* and no real harm done. A chance combination of other small miscalculations on my part, however, and Beever's astute snatching at opportunity came together to produce an enormity of unparalleled proportion. I was totally unprepared for the toilet paper in the bathtub.

Once before I had come home to find the tub filled with toilet paper—yards and yards of it—but that was different because the paper had been dry. Following that first incident, in which it had been Goop who was the transgressor, I removed the temptation by transferring the roll from its receptacle in the wall to a new location out of reach on the barricaded sink. (Okee, incidentally, never to my knowledge ever bothered the paper in the Wisbeskis' bathroom despite its accessibility.) Beever eventually learned how to poke his muzzle around the sink barricade—just enough to nudge the roll into the basin, where a dripping faucet would make it useless—so the usual resting-place of the roll became the ledge at the rear of the sink, a place not terribly convenient but at least safe. Once in a while I would forget to replace the roll after taking a length of paper to wipe my eyeglasses just before leaving for work in the morning, and on this morning I had left the roll within reach. I had also left three or four inches of water in the tub for the otter, something I had done only a few times before. In the past the water had leaked out slowly during the day, giving the otter a few hours for sloshing around. This time the water didn't leak away and I was greeted by a sea of lavender liquid. Beever had somehow managed not to nudge the roll of paper out of reach, but pulled it down instead and carried the purple tissue into the tub before unraveling it. Once wet the paper couldn't unwind, and Beever must have bitten and clawed off huge unresisting chunks of pulp which neither sank nor floated but merely hung suspended in the water, fragmenting and separating into smaller flakes as he frolicked in the mess.

At my first sight of the tub I stood staring in dumb incomprehension for a second, perhaps much less, and in that brief moment before recognition came and I comprehended the nature of the slop before me, two thoughts reeled through my mind. During my childhood in Jersey City there had been a devout Jewish family a few doors away who made wine every Passover season, and I recalled having watched some of the process. The stuff in the bathtub, except for its paler tint, suggested the pulpy residue of the squeezed grapes. Even more it made me think insanely of curdled purple milk, and Gelett Burgess's infamous Purple Cow.

For what seemed a very long time (and probably was) I just stood there absorbing the situation, not yet bold enough to begin making plans for restoring the tub to its proper condition. Draining the tub I could see was not the answer, unless I wanted the trap filled with papier-mâché; it was obvious that the paper pulp had to be separated from the water before either could be removed, and that was the problem. After searching the cellar for a scrap of wire screening and finding none I took one of the narrow casement window screens, only to discover that it was just an inch or so too wide to fit the bottom of the tub. A kind of numb panic took hold of me as I contemplated removing the pulp by hand, which it occurred to me would be a somewhat tedious and impractical undertaking. Beever chose that instant to slither into the tub and when he raised his head his whiskers were lavender, festooned with clinging pulp. As in most otter atrocities this superfluous touch of slapstick worked the magical effect of snapping me out of my dumb horror and reduced me to helpless and perhaps just a trifle hysterical laughter.

From this point on, my mind began functioning effectively again and I remembered that there was some sort of colander in the kitchen. What I found was not really a colander but a flat container like a cake pan, with holes in the central part of the bottom. It served the purpose after a fashion, but each load had to be sloshed back and forth the way a miner in the old West panned for gold. It was ghastly, slow work. To this day I have no idea what the pan was originally intended for, but I keep it handy along with a real colander that I purchased the next day,

and which I have never used for preparing food or, fortunately, for any other purpose. It's just reassuring to know that the things are around.

Newspapers were Beever's other passion, under the proper circumstances. He learned without difficulty to urinate and defecate on spread newspaper, a feat which required no tutoring on my part beyond placing the paper at the spot he chose as a latrine. Papers spread in any other location never inspired him to this end—in fact he ignored them. This had its advantages, for the Sunday papers on the floor were perfectly safe, but contrariwise he steadfastly refused to move his latrine when I moved the papers to a place less inconvenient to me than the bathroom doorway. Folded newspapers, however, Beever found irresistible. It was my custom to stack the papers for several days at the far end of the sofa, to my left as I sat. While I was otherwise occupied, usually in reading, Beever, lying on his back next to me, would stretch over and languidly tear off the corners of the papers. My usual response was to reach out my left hand and drag him by the tail toward me and away from the papers, and in time I developed the ability to perform the act almost unconsciously. It goes without saying that as soon as I went back to whatever I had been doing Beever would return to what he had been doing, until the session ended with a cuffing or a puff of cigarette smoke in his face, accompanied more often than not by a few select expletives from my rich vocabulary. Beever's efforts produced a steady accretion of inch-wide paper scraps that grew until even my unfinicky nature compelled me to resort to the vacuum cleaner. By that time there was normally a wealth of shed fennec fuzz about as well, and the belated housecleaning served a double purpose.

The best description I can find for our relationship is that Beever and I were friends, as much as a human and nonhuman can be. As in a real friendship between humans, we had a strong bond of mutual trust. Again, it's difficult to avoid anthropomorphic terms, and when I speak of the otter's "trust" I don't mean a conscious state of self-imposed vulnerability of the sort that I placed in Beever after a careful appraisal of his behavior, but something akin to the blind trust of a child, conscious, perhaps, but only barely—in some dim way, a precursor of what has flowered in the vastly more complex human mind. There have been two dogs in my life who trusted me implicitly; my affection for them was not at all diminished by the fact that such trust is a part of a dog's genetic heritage, nurtured for centuries, perhaps millennia, of selective breeding by human masters. I expected trust and affection from the dogs, but I could not in the same sense expect such feelings from Beever, whose ancestors were wild, free-living creatures hunted by humans for as long as there have been men in Colombia. At most I had hoped for a tractable nature in this cub who had drawn his first breath in a river-bank den and who had doubtless been captured with no little trauma.

Beever's powers of forbearance toward discipline were a constant source of surprise to me. He bore blows so hard that at times my fingers throbbed for the better part of a half hour. He bore such flat-handed blows without retaliation and amended his ways for only as long as the lesson could override his inborn otter exuberance.

Disciplining an otter is no easy task. You can forget the mechanics of training a dog, rolled-up newspaper and all. Symbolic taps Beever ignored completely, and the most severe blows I could force myself to administer barely conveyed their intended message. Not that he was stupid—perish the thought. The same principles that one uses to train a dog apply to an otter but the implementation differs greatly in a quantitative way and, to a degree, qualitatively as well. To begin with, an otter seems to be made entirely of gristle and sinew—anything short of violence he ignores simply because it doesn't hurt. A dog is far more sensitive to pain (at least this is my impression) but, more important, a dog's psyche is geared to obedience and an otter's is not. A dog is by nature a social animal; an otter is a *sociable* one. A *social* animal (like the dog) is one which normally lives in a group of a fairly stable nature, with a more or less well-defined hierarchy. A wild-dog pack has a dominant animal, the leader, and an underdog, with other members ranged between the extremes. To a domestic dog the human family is the "pack" and he is the lowest member. He accepts his role, in part through affability and partly because he is usually much the smallest member of the group. (Many an unprovoked attack by a large dog upon family members is probably an attempt at social climbing.) The otter is, by my definition, a *sociable* animal—one that does not live in a true, or structured, society. Otters like company and there are innumerable accounts of otters meeting and stopping to frolic when they meet in the course of their wanderings. Sometimes several hunt and play together for a time, and there almost certainly exists some sort of peck-order at such times, but these companies seem loosely organized at best, and generally impermanent.

A dog can adopt a subservient role by nature, but an otter is a natural-born hedonist, and his joyous obsession with living the present to the fullest gives him a cavalier disregard for tedious things like rules of conduct. There is little to suggest that otters form their occasional groups for the purpose of hunting in concert, which seems to be a principal reason behind the more permanent social structure of lions and wolves, for example. Certainly two or more otters may hunt simultaneously in the same place, and perhaps their joint presence may prove more successful than if they hunted singly. But the psychology of cooperative hunting demands a prey large enough to require a cooperative approach and, more important, large enough to feed the hunter group. By and large the otter's food consists of morsels—crayfish, frogs, and small bottom-fish—none large enough to share, as a rule. (I have never heard of an otter, other than a mother weaning her cubs, willingly sharing its food.) If the procurement of food, then, is not the basis of otter companionship, the only reason apparent to me is the sport and sociability that contact with their fellows provides.

When I try to analyze the reasons for Beever's supreme good will toward me, I find myself at a loss for any certain answer. Certainly all of his predecessors had behaved amiably toward me, but then they had all been cubs and none had lived as much as a month before succumbing to the disease I came to dread so deeply. Beever, who escaped this damnable disease only for a time, lived with me for not quite a year. During this time he enjoyed greater freedom with my person and belongings than any of the otters before him, but in at least equal measure he was subject to a far greater degree of discipline than the others. Not that he ever became truly disciplined; he could never be trusted with a tub of water for an entire day, nor could he be expected to respect the contents of any cabinet he had once learned to open. The clutter atop my desk was safe only because he could not climb to it, and eventually, after he found out how to push the drawers out from behind with his nose and then use them as steps, the top of the desk and all its motley treasures were his. But in things that mattered I could not have asked for a more benign familiar. Beever's transgressions were, as far as I can tell, always purely a matter of oversight on his part—or a lack of foresight on mine.

Guilt as we conceive of it has no existence in the mind of an animal. The animal's innocence, like a human infant's, is a negative thing, unborn because the mind lacks any ability to discern good from evil, lacks the intricacy to relate its own immediate well-being with something external to itself—even with its own well-being in the long run. When the dentist says, "This is going to hurt a little," you and I, whether we do it in an elaborately evident way or not (taking that "little" with a wry inner smile), accept the coming pain because we believe that it will prevent a future pain of greater magnitude and duration. Pain in any form is evil, and is the only form in which evil impinges upon the animal mind. An animal avoids pain at all costs; beyond that, anything that is pleasurable is good, and is not only acceptable but desirable. We humans, guided by our ability to grasp things in the abstract and to project ourselves into the future, forgo certain pleasurable experiences because of their future consequences. As kids we refrained from one enjoyable act or another for no other reason than parental ordinance and the consequences of disobedience. Still, there were times when the sight of the icing on a cake cooling on the kitchen table somehow became a present good that overrode all other considerations and a fingerful just *had* to be sampled.

All of Beever's peccadillos fell into this last category. Some of them were atrocities of outrageous proportions so much larger than life that I invariably burst into laughter in spite of myself. Other, far lesser ones, perpetrated usually at times when my resistance was low, evoked violent reactions from me. Three o'clock in the morning is no time for an otter to begin racing around on the bed of a man who has to rise at seven to get to work on time, and it's doubly precarious for the otter to be dealt with by one whose temperate qualities are slower to awaken than his righteous indignation. Perhaps this was why Beever learned most quickly and lastingly that bedtime meant sleeping time, because in such periods I responded in a more nearly true animal fashion, less tempered by compassion than when I was fully awake.

8   The Deadly, That We Thought Were Dead

Beever's doom was sealed on the fourth of June, the day I brought home another otter. I had given a good deal of thought to the purchase, arriving at the decision to add a second otter to the household only after setting up what I thought were adequate safeguards. My prime concern was the disease that had killed Beever's predecessors, the identity of which was still far from certain. I knew by now that the first month was crucial and that any new otter would have to be quarantined for at least that length of time. As it happened, the dealer had a young female which had been at his establishment for six months. I felt certain that his store had harbored the disease, and the knowledge that he had kept an otter there in good health for six months was reason to hope that the danger had been eliminated. On the other hand an otter that had not been handled for so long was likely not to be very tame.

There were two reasons for buying a second otter. First, I felt that I had not been able to give Beever all the attention he needed, and another otter would make a far better wrestling companion than I could. Second, I hoped to observe the behavior of a female, and that of the two as a pair, with at least a small hope that their association might result in cubs. Two otters, I understand from my reading, never become as good with a person as a single animal does, but I reasoned that Beever's attachment to me was by now very strong and probably permanent, so I worried little about the situation. I hoped that the female, even if she were not tame, would attach herself to Beever and through him might come to terms with me. When she arrived I had a name already chosen for her—Tinca, a pleasant-sounding name of a genus of fish.

Tinca was well-grown, weighing nine and a half pounds. From above she looked like a small edition of Beever, except that the four outer fingers of her left forepaw were clothed in white hair. What her underside looked like I could not tell, because she was unwilling to allow me a close approach. Released in the living room (Beever was locked in his half of the house), she wandered warily about and, before I knew what had happened, disappeared. I searched all of the likely hiding places, then such unlikely ones as the space behind and under the kitchen range. Only by accident did I think of looking in the one place in which none of my animals had ever hidden.

For two years I had been storing some furniture belonging to an old friend who hired out for a two-year tour teaching high school for the Army in Europe. Two of the items were an excellent radio-phonograph console and a television set, both rather expensive, and under our agreement I made free use of both. The third piece was an ornate chest of drawers with gracefully curved lines, and a base enclosed in front and on the sides. I cared little for it because I have no enthusiasm for the ornate, and it was horribly out of place among the stark rectangular forms of my own furniture; still, I kept it in the living room, thinking this to be the safest place. (When at last my friend reclaimed his belongings I found that Pixie had at some time lifted his leg against it and the base was discolored, with its veneer beginning to peel—Dick was very good about it all.) Tinca was hiding under the chest. I flushed her out, and went at last to fetch Beever.

Again I had forgotten to place the plywood on the air conditioner, and Beever was in bed, accompanied by the usual disarray. Following my custom for introducing animals, I got Beever into his wire traveling crate and set it out in the living room. Tinca seemed not to know he was there, and after a while I gently walked her into another wire crate. When I freed Beever he in turned appeared oblivious to the female, but after a few minutes he noticed her. Approaching the crate warily he pushed his muzzle against it, whiskers pointed forward, and briefly the two otters stood with their vibrissae meshed. Tinca uttered a low, moaning growl similar to the one Beever reserved for visitors, but he was not to be put off. Soon he began the staccato chittering he had made when he met Okee, and pushed his paws through the wire. Otherwise nothing much happened. Just before Beever first spied Tinca's cage I had been sitting next to it (thinking that if he came to me he would find her) and the little female had been quiet, accepting meat from my fingers and even permitting me to stroke her cheek with my finger. Because she had earlier given the alarm "Hah!" when I walked nearby, I had been holding my foot against the wire, and she was growing accustomed to it. When nothing of consequence followed Beever's initial greeting I released Tinca. She waddled out, and Beever dashed after her. In the next instant she was the pursuer, and for perhaps fifteen minutes the two

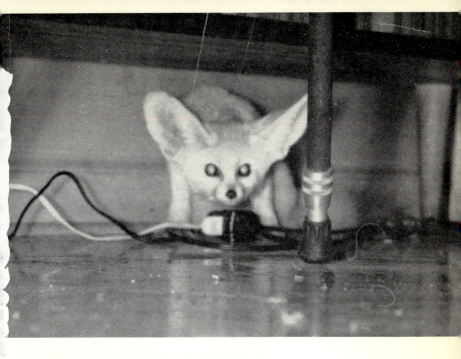

Pixie

The Otterproof toilet

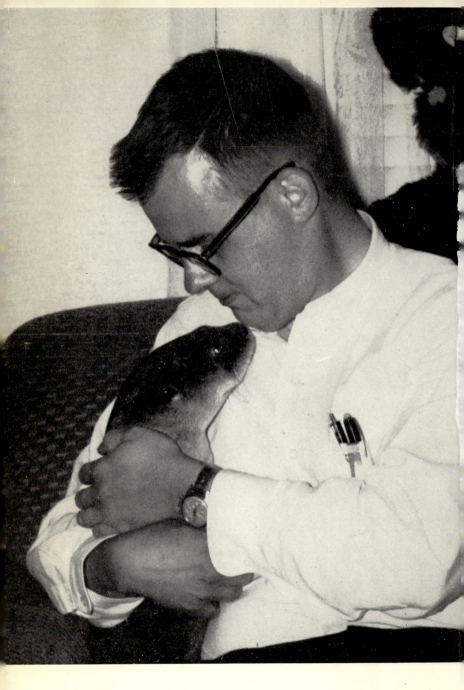

Beever and friend

raced around the room, tumbling and twisting, with not a sign of hostility and with very little vocalization. Several times Beever leaped at her and sank his teeth into her with the snake-like striking movement he used on me in play, but Tinca never complained. At last Beever ran off to dunk his head in the water bowl in the next room, and then climbed up onto the sofa next to me, where he rolled over on his back. He lay there a long time with his mouth open, panting heavily. His entire body seemed to take part in the panting, with his belly quivering like gelatin and ripples flowing rearward, giving the silvery fur the appearance of a breeze-rippled field of sere grass. Twice more the two otters chased one another, and each time the game ended by mutual consent.

All this time Tinca was incubating her distemper without showing a symptom. I could never get the dealer to admit it, but he must have imported a diseased ocelot or margay just before delivering the otter, and her six months of health came to an end.

On the tenth of June, a Monday, I brought Tinca and Pixie to the Zoo, the otter to be cared for while I traveled westward for a month-long vacation of sorts and Pix to remain permanently. The fennec found a congenial life with two others of his kind in the Small Mammal House, but he remembered me and would accord me a slightly more fervent growl than he did his keepers. That night Dorothy Reville came to call for the two bush-babies I was minding while she and her husband vacationed in Trinidad. I was far from sad to see them go. The smaller of the two, known as a Demidoff's bushbaby and christened Ignatz, had been something of a distraction. I knew from books that these diminutive primates filled the West African forests with nocturnal calling, but not until I was settling into bed that first night, having just switched off the light, did I conceive

I

even faintly the volume or maniacal quality of the call. Even after two weeks it unsettled me.

On the day before, I had taken Beever to South Bound Brook, where the Wisbeskis were to keep him until my return. He recognized Luke, Dotty, and Okee immediately, and when I left that evening I knew he was in good hands. As I prepared to enter my car Beever was playing on the lawn with Luke. I went over to give him a last pat on the head before departing, and Beever scarcely looked up at me. There was no frantic attempt to follow me, no anguished farewell. My last sight of Beever alive gladdened me at the time, because I knew he would be kept too busy to miss me.

Jack Schoenherr and I left for the West on Wednesday, the twelfth of June, in my Volkswagen, loaded down with more baggage than we ever got to use. We had planned a loose itinerary with two principal stops, the meetings of the American Society of Mammalogists at Albuquerque (with a visit to my friend Ivo Poglayen who was then director of the small zoo there) and Point Lobos, California, where Jack and I hoped to observe and photograph sea otters. Jack and I had met not quite a year earlier at the Zoo, where he had come to deliver illustrations for a brochure Dorothy Reville was working on. Jack is a talented artist whose principal work at that time had been in science fiction (he once did a cover for *Astounding Science Fiction* magazine showing a curiously convincing extraterrestrial catlike beast that was green and six-legged). Since then he has broadened his field to include a good deal of real-animal paintings, particularly of the big cats, and his illustrations in books, most notable *Rascal*, have brought him well-deserved praise. His participation in the long journey had a twofold purpose: I had sold him on photographing the sea otters, and he also wanted to photograph rocky, bleak, Western landscapes, some of which have long since turned up in unearthly disguise on the covers of *Analog*, the publication that has been metamorphosed from the old *Astounding*.

Jack and I have a great many common interests, but the protocol of automobile travel is not one of them. Although we both normally do our best work in the late evening hours and function poorly in the hours before noon, on long trips I reverse my pattern, primarily in order to be sure of finding lodgings at motels along the way. On the second afternoon out I discovered to my horror that Jack wanted to drive well on into the night, a practice that was more than once to force us to sleep in roach-infested motels or, if we were lucky, decent places with only a single bed available, so that one of us spent the night sleeping on the floor.

Our first real stop was at Kansas City, where I wanted to visit the late Art Hoffman, a retired automobile dealer from whom most of the zoos in this country bought their North American otters. The Hoffmans lived in a most beautiful rambling ranch house on an enormous spread of land, with a pond downslope from the house. If the house and grounds were not enough to incite me to envy, a large rectangular wire enclosure occupied by about a dozen otters was. The structure was compartmented into several pens of various sizes, each with snug nest boxes, and most had a swimming tank. A roof sheltered the whole thing. Art had sunk some large galvanized cattle troughs in the lawn outside a huge picture window; in the breeding season portable pens would be set up around each trough and a pair of otters introduced, while Art watched from indoors to ascertain whether breeding took place or not. Since he had experienced a heart attack a few years earlier and of necessity had to curtail his own activity, this arrangement worked well. Art and Mrs. Hoffman had kept otters in their house some years ago but there was no longer any sign of their presence, and Art's contact with the animals had once been greater. Now, for this thriving group he employed a full-time otter handler, whom we saw in one of the pens with a "tame" male. Art's idea of tameness differed a little from mine; actually the otter *was* tame, but just a little rough in his play. The otter was obviously overjoyed at having human company, jumping up against the man like a dog. But before the handler left the pen small trickles of blood issued from both hands and his cheek, where the otter's enthusiasm had led him to nip too vigorously. I remember thinking that Beever would have done the same had I not continually reminded him manually of the permissible limits of his dental exercise. I did not know that Tinca had died at the Zoo some time during that night and that, as I stood watching Art Hoffman's otters, Beever was beginning to show symptoms of the disease in the Wisbeski household.

On the day of our departure Keeper Bob Mahoney found that Tinca had not eaten Tuesday's meal. Animals go off feed occasionally, and he did not worry, beyond sending a stool specimen to the Animal Hospital for examination. I had quartered Tinca in the old nursery of the Lion House, a room that contains two large cages sometimes used for the big cats if they have to be removed temporarily from exhibition. One cage was occupied by Chipper, the Panama otter belonging to the Education Department. Tinca was installed in the unoccupied adjoining cage. Bob kept detailed notes on the otter's progress, and the following account is a brief summary of what happened.

After sending the stool sample to the hospital Bob offered Tinca her morning meal, which she refused. At noon he placed in the cage a wooden trough with a ramp, and Tinca plunged into it immediately, stretching out on the ramp later for a nap.

Later he sat in the cage, speaking softly and attempting to hand-feed her, but she was unresponsive, and when after an hour she began to growl, he left, not wishing to overstay his welcome. He left the afternoon feeding of chopped meat, cubes of whole meat, and half of a hard-boiled egg. On the following morning the whole meat, the egg, and half of the chopped meat were gone.

Tinca allowed Bob to sit with her again in the afternoon, lying on her ramp and showing mild interest in his presence. When Chipper was returned from his daily school lecture-trip Tinca awakened from her nap and walked past Bob to the front of the cage to investigate. She again refused food but ate some of the whole meat and egg during the night, before she died. On Friday morning she was dead, her body relaxed, with no visible sign of a violent passing. No blood had been noted in her stool and apparently she had not vomited; Bob mentioned no diarrhea, but then such a condition would be difficult to see in the normally fluid stool of a meat-fed otter. Shortly afterward Chipper grew ill, but ultimately pulled through.

Meanwhile Jack and I were incommunicado, pushing westward as rapidly as one can in a Volkswagen. We arrived at the University of New Mexico in Albuquerque late on Sunday afternoon. Beever had grown steadily worse, and Dotty called the Zoo the next morning. Someone from my office tried to reach me, but the message arrived while I was attending the morning session of the meetings in another part of the campus and reached me only after lunch. When I called Dotty she filled me in on what had been happening—I was stunned by the news. There was nothing I could do to help. The veterinarian in attendance was an excellent one and Beever had found trustworthy friends in the Wisbeskis. I was in touch several times during the day; Dotty suggested that I fly back to comfort my otter, but I couldn't make a plane connection before late Tuesday or Wednesday morning because Albuquerque was not on a heavily traveled air route.

When I called for the last time on Monday evening the sound of distress was absent from Dotty's voice as she told me how Beever had awakened from a deep sleep greatly improved in spirit. From her manner of speech I could tell that she felt that the crisis had passed and that the otter would soon be well. Hope is often an insidious thing but it can serve as temporary relief from an oppressive burden. I elected not to tell Dotty and Luke that their optimism would be short-lived, that in feline enteritis seeming recovery is a characteristic event that presages the end, and that death was lurking near for Beever. I dreaded my phone call in the morning, knowing what had probably already happened, and when Luke answered instead of Dotty, whatever tenacious vestiges of hope were still mine vanished. Luke said hello and then there was a long silence. When he spoke again he was weeping, this huge bear of a man. I had had almost a day to resign myself to Beever's death; the thousands of miles that separated me from it made it no less vivid, for through the night I relived in my mind the last moments of Goop and Joey, and my imagination superimposed Beever's much more familiar personality upon those agonies. But I had not been prepared to face Luke's reaction to the event; somehow I tried to reassure him and to sound more resigned to the tragedy than I really was. I will never be able to forget the awful moments of that conversation and the knowledge that death had not only claimed my otter—who had made himself "my" otter more than any proprietary right of mine ever could —but had desolated Luke and Dotty as well.

9 The Supine Mariners

The remainder of the Mammal Society meetings has faded from my memory. I know that I presented a paper, and that for a while at least I attended the presentation of other papers, but most of the time I sought solitude, and Jack respected my unspoken wish.

Hobart Van Deusen of the American Museum of Natural History joined us on the next leg of our journey, with stops at the Museum's research station in the Chiricahua Mountains of Arizona, the Phoenix Zoo (in time to see the arrival of the group of Arabian oryxes, whose future in captivity may be the only future left to the species), and the Arizona-Sonora Desert Museum. My two companions did a great deal to divert my mind from Beever's passing, and by the time we left Van at the airport in Tucson I had convinced myself that I was again taking an interest in things. Jack and I pressed on for a visit to the

San Diego Zoo, then north along the California coast to Point Lobos.

* * *

The guidebook calls it "the greatest meeting of land and water in the world"; the map more prosaically calls it Point Lobos, and it juts into the Pacific Ocean some eighty miles south of San Francisco. In an age of careless superlatives, the guidebook phrase is easy to shrug off—unless you have been there. Our ultimate goal had been to feast our sight on sea otters along the coast. Although sea otters have occurred from Washington south to Baja California, the Monterey area, and particularly Point Lobos, is one of the best places to see them.

Point Lobos Reserve State Park is a model of careful planning and continuing meticulous attention to its objectives. Minute in size for a state park (the Reserve comprises 354 acres, only about half again as large as the New York Zoological Park), strictly enforced regulations governing its use have preserved the wild character of the land. Vehicular roads are reduced to a minimum, and most of the park can be reached only by narrow footpaths which are seldom visible as you scan the landscape. Camping is forbidden, for even the most experienced camper cannot help leaving long-lasting traces of his presence.

We were more fortunate than most visitors to the Reserve. Chuck Maddock, the Ranger at the entrance gate, broke into a broad grin when he heard that I came from the Bronx Zoo. He had grown up in New Jersey, and had visited the Zoo often. From this chance encounter came an invitation for us to stay as Chuck's guests at his home within the Reserve. This was the Whaler's Cottage, an ancient low-slung structure almost hidden between two enormous Monterey cypresses. The cottage floor tilted up noticeably at both ends, pried up by the inexorably growing roots of the trees outside, but a canted bed was a small price to pay for the companionship of two such magnificent trees.

Point Lobos is characterized by a mild year-round temperature, frequent fogs, and high winds off the ocean. The most conspicuous testimonial to the winds is the rugged response of the cypresses, which have appealed to painters for so long. But other and more subtle effects can be seen. The weather is one. Grinnell and Linsdale, two zoologists who surveyed the site in the thirties, remarked that by jutting into the sea the Point became nearly independent of the mainland's influence on its weather, so that the variations in one day's weather may be nearly as great as its range throughout an entire year. The Point Lobos fogs certainly enhance the aesthetic qualities of the landscape, but we were fortunate in not having to cope with them during the period of our otter-watching.

The rocks of the Point are of two kinds. A hard granite, that can be seen at its most spectacular where the sea has carved it at Cypress Headland, appears to be the basic rock of the Point. At Sea Lion Point, where we spent most of our time, the rock is of a vastly different sort. Here it is a conglomerate of comparatively recent origin. Bits of the granite and other rocks, fallen into the sea and ground by waves and sand, have become mixed with the sand and gravel of the shore and hardened into a weak sandstone. This conglomerate then rose above the waters to be eroded again into cliffs. The exposed surfaces look and feel like an overly sandy concrete fill, studded with oval stones of muted greens, purples, and pinks and carved into bizarre hollows and projections. Within these jagged hollows Jack and I hid, observing the otters until we discovered that we could expose ourselves to view without alarming them.

Flights of sea birds met our eyes almost constantly during our two days along the shore. Cormorants of two species, black silhouettes against the sea, kept a continuous shuttle up and down the coast, flying low above the water. Small groups of brown pelicans came by frequently, alternately flapping with slow, majestic strokes and gliding on stiffened wings. Pigeon guillemots hurtled down from the cliff to bob in the water like small black-and-white ducks, or took flight in a frenzy of wingbeats that seemed at first to be more a valiant effort than successful flight. Occasionally after peering through the spotting scope for a while we would idly scan the shoreline rocks to rest our eyes. Often our attention was caught by a small scarlet bar resting horizontally against the dark rock. Scrutinized through binoculars the red bar would become a bill attached to a black oyster catcher. Later, following the flight of one of these birds, we were still surprised at how instantly and completely the bird disappeared when it came to rest, save for the bill.

The offshore rocks harbor colonies of Steller's sea lions, one of the largest species of eared seal, and the deep, rumbling, belch-like calls of the bulls were clearly audible over the sound of the surf. The smaller California sea lions were present in lesser numbers, mere remnants of a larger herd that had already left for its breeding and pupping grounds to the south. Occasionally harbor seals could be seen along the shore, but they were inconspicuous. The seals themselves are fascinating animals and would have repaid full-time study, but we were concentrating on the otters and our principal interest in the seals lay in their interactions with the otters.

On the headland above Sea Lion Point the chaparral gives way to mats of bluff lettuce, fleshy plants that reminded me of the hen-and-chickens in my own rock garden, but which had translucent, pink, upright stems rising from the leafy base. The bluff lettuce was in flower when we set up our watch on the Point, its yellow flowers surrounded by questing bees. With such a superabundance of natural beauty to lead the eye and the other senses on to closer attention, Point Lobos Reserve would be an inexhaustible source for wonder and delight even if there were no sea otters. But there were sea otters, and these were what we had come to observe.

We arrived at Point Lobos Reserve State Park late in the afternoon of the last day in June and saw our first sea otter that evening, toward dusk. The Park naturalist, Judson Vandevere, had offered to show us where the otters were likely to be and I, at least, followed him with a familiar feeling of pessimism born of having followed other people who were going to show me some prized species or other. Jud had made no promises, though, and perhaps that was why an otter was there. Despite the failing light I stood literally entranced by the sight of a large otter far below us in the cove to our left. It floated on its back, holding on its chest a large abalone on which it dined in a leisurely and almost dainty manner, finally discarding the shell.

It is this side of the sea otter's personality that has caused it some trouble in the area, for the abalone fishermen are jealous and possessive where the big shellfish is concerned. In truth, the otters eat relatively few abalone, but when they do they leave telltale evidence behind in the form of a characteristic missing piece from almost every shell that lies on the ocean floor. Mussels and sea urchins form the bulk of the otters' diet and, to the zoologist, the more interesting part.

We were able to spend two more days and part of the third watching the sea otters but, short as the time was, it was enough to reveal a good deal about the life of the animals, particularly for a comparison of their behavior with that of the river otters. Among other things, it brought into doubt a remark made by Ernest Thompson Seton about sea otters and Steller's sea lions.

Like all writers, myself included, Seton, despite his broad personal familiarity with so many of the North American mammals, was often forced to rely on the reports of others, and when he accepted a story of the predation of the sea lion on otters he had, I suspect, been sold a bill of goods. Seton listed Steller's sea lion as a major predator upon the sea otter, but in less than three days we saw numerous instances of Stellers swimming within a few feet of otters. Mother otters with cubs paid no more than the most casual attention to the big seals, and single otters eating mussels and urchins continued to munch placidly as the sea lions' heads cut the water nearby. These observations do not by any means disprove Seton's allegation, but if sea lions preyed upon otters to any extent at all one would expect the otters to display just a bit less nonchalance in the face of a potential enemy. (Professor Barabash-Nikiforov writes of the creatures in Russian waters: "When swimming sea otters and sea lions meet, each quietly ignores the other.")

Sea otters are in many ways the most aberrant of otters. They are the largest members, in terms of mass, of the weasel family. The giant otter of South America attains a greater length (claimed to be nearly seven feet from the nose to the tip of the tail) but, based upon the weight of a female at the Bronx Zoo, the males, which are larger, probably do not reach even seventy pounds—the only published weight I can find for a male is fifty-three pounds (the Zoo's female weighed fifty pounds, six ounces). Sea otters grow to about five feet or so but have short tails for otters, and are known to reach nearly eighty pounds. Their hind feet are relatively enormous, and unlike all other species have toes that grow longer from the inner side of the foot to the outer edge. This characteristic, with webs that extend to the ends of the toes, gives the hind foot the appearance of a seal's rear flipper. By contrast, the sea otter's forepaw looks like little more than a stump. Seen from above, the fingers seem to have been amputated, and only on the underside can indentations be found that correspond (nearly) to finger separations, but one of these is actually two fingers, bearing on its upper surface two inconspicuous claws rather than one. There is, however, no webbing between the fingers, nor in fact any functional separation.* Yet the otter uses this clumsy-looking club-footed hand with dexterity, and does things with it that no other otter species does. It uses these functionally unfingered paws as hands to hold its food and, more remarkably, to break open mollusks by hammering them on stones brought to the surface for the purpose. But it is another characteristic that caused trouble for the species. The sea otter has fur so prized that it nearly caused the otter's extinction at the hands of man. In 1910 a single pelt, the last one taken by legal means prior to an international ban on hunting, brought almost two thousand dollars.

In 1737 Padre Taraval saw the first sea otters at Cedros Island off the coast of Baja California, but did not publish the discovery for twenty years. Meanwhile in 1741 Vitus Bering discovered, and spent time on, the island that bears his name. On the beach and in the kelp beds offshore he saw "droves" of otters, and in short order he and his men killed "upward of 800 of

---

* Here is a magnificent example of how misinformation can be perpetuated, and I have left the statement in the text to expiate my scientific sin. I was repeating, without citing its author, an inaccuracy. In April 1968, when this manuscript had been sent to the publisher, I had an opportunity to spend several days observing sea otters from within their enclosure at Seattle's Woodland Park Zoo, where I got several excellent close-up views of the otters manipulating objects. Perhaps it would not be precise to say now that true webs exist between the fingers, but the otters *are* capable of spreading the fingers, and the skin between them does stretch. In spite of the clumsy appearance of the hands and the seeming non-existence of usable fingers, the latter are in fact remarkably functional. *Mea culpa!*

them and if the narrow limits of the craft we constructed had permitted, we should have killed three times as many."

One hundred and sixty-nine years later the sea otter existed only in a few tattered bands in the northern waters. Only small numbers of the California herd were seen after the first decade of this century, and a group of thirty-one otters noted in 1916 was the largest aggregation recorded for some time. Thereafter few otters were seen for more than thirty years.

A proposal was made in this country in 1874 to regulate sea otter hunting because of the imminence of the species' doom. The year 1911 finally saw passage of an international treaty, and with painful slowness the sea otter has been increasing since that time.

On 19 March, 1938, the California herd made its official reappearance as a herd; a group estimated (perhaps overestimated) at 400 individuals was sighted a few miles south of Carmel, on the Monterey Peninsula. Thereafter careful counts showed the herd to number something under a hundred otters—still the largest aggregation known for a generation, at least. Rigid conservation measures have protected these animals, but the otters' low reproductive rate has made their comeback a slow one. A recent survey places their population off California at about 650.

Jack and I confined our observations to Sea Lion Point itself and two adjacent coves, so we never saw the entire population of the area. The herd we spent most of our time with numbered about twenty. An accurate count was difficult for us, as beginners, for two reasons. First, the gas-filled bladders of the kelp, which float on the surface, look very much like otter heads at a distance—they brought back memories of my turtle-hunting youth when the heads of my quarry and water-lily buds were a problem to distinguish at times. Still, with only a few hours of observation we began to improve in our ability to spot the real otters. The other problem, also a function of distance, was that during the Park's visiting hours the otters resting at the far edge of the kelp beds were indistinct even with a 60X scope, and we may have missed a few cubs riding on their mothers' chests. Only after the Reserve closed its gates did otters approach the shore, other than an occasional one that might come into a cove but was still well away from the shore.

The distant kelp beds were bands of gently heaving glass, subduing the incoming waves within their confines, only to relinquish their effect as the waves passed them on the way to the shore. Within the tranquillity of the kelp beds the otters spent their time in seeming languor under the maritime sun—"loitering" was the word that came to mind. Some were apparently asleep or resting, while others groomed themselves in a leisurely fashion, and the females cared for their cubs.

In the short time we spent at Point Lobos we were able to recognize several individual otters. Early on our first morning a large otter with the straw-colored head of an adult moved into Whalers' Cove. As she dozed in the kelp (the determination of sex was tentative, but based on the ease with which river otters may be sexed at a distance when on their backs), she turned her head toward us, revealing a bright pink nose that must have been old scar tissue in view of its asymmetrical shape. For about ten minutes she floated on her back, assuming many poses that we think of as alien to nonhumans. She crossed her flipperlike hind feet over her abdomen, rested one forepaw on her nose, and closed her eyes. From time to time she opened her eyes to look about or to groom the fur on her arm, but mostly she just dozed. Meanwhile a second otter, a male, perhaps a nearly full-sized cub, appeared and approached Pinky (she had acquired a name by now). The male began by poking about Pinky's head and shoulders. She took the intrusion calmly, and for a while both animals floated together, each occasionally rolling through a full turn. During one early roll we noticed a small pink scar on the edge of the left hind foot of the male—in a long-term study such an individual distinguishing characteristic would be useful. For half an hour the two otters stayed near one another, each diving below the surface momentarily, to reappear with a morsel of food (probably sea urchins, although we could not tell) and eat it. At one point Pinky reached forward with one hind foot to scratch at her neck; then she put her left forepaw behind her neck in an appealingly human manner and floated there with her elbow jutting outward and upward. She tucked her chin down into her chest and closed her eyes. The male crossed his wrists on his chest and like the female dozed off.

For the next two days I watched and photographed the otters, and I found myself regretting desperately that we had no tape recorder. It is almost impossible to write notes and at the same time keep a telescope trained on an otter. Even though the animals moved about comparatively little, the rise and fall of the waves made it necessary to keep both hands occupied in maneuvering the scope. I missed a good deal of what was happening because of this but even so gained a far broader picture of sea otter behavior than I had expected. The more I have read about the species since that day, the more I have found that most, if not all, of our observations have been made and published by others before us, but the exultation of discovery I felt as each of the facets of the otters' behavior revealed itself has a value to me that transcends all other considerations.

Most of our observations during the day were of otters lolling at some distance out, but from about five o'clock through the three hours until sunset a number of otters approached the shoreline, in a few cases to within five feet of our rock promontory in the rolling surf. Through much of the first afternoon we crouched in the weirdly sculptured hollows of the rock, only our eyes, the cameras, or the telescope showing. The sharp knife-edges of the rock made our vigil most uncomfortable, but it is a measure of the fascination of otter-watching that truthfully we were aware of our discomfort only when the otters were quiescent. Later, things got easier. Just how it happened neither of us remembers, but we found ourselves standing in full view of an otter we had not noticed before. The animal was only a few yards from shore, and although it was aware of our presence it accorded us a total indifference. From then on our work was not limited by topography, and we were able to move freely to the best vantage points whenever our subject moved.

With our new mobility we were able to see other things, too. Although we saw otters eating sea urchins and an occasional abalone, by far the commonest item of their diet was mussels. Twice Jack saw an otter getting mussels from the base of a partly exposed rock in the cove. The tide was coming in by that time and the small portion of the rock still above water was awash with each new wave. As the trough passed, exposing the rock below waterline, Jack saw an otter at the mussel bed grasping a mussel in both forepaws (we had wondered whether paws or teeth were used to dislodge the mollusks), but the mussel clung tenaciously to its rock. As the crest of the next wave swept by, the otter held fast to its prey as its hind feet and tail swayed with the water's movement. Several successive waves moved by, sweeping the otter's hindmost parts like a strand of kelp, each trough revealing that it still grasped its mussel. Then the otter surfaced with its booty.

The otters' method of opening mussels is the sort of thing that has been well documented in print, but it must be wit-

K

nessed to be fully appreciated. Until I saw the procedure myself I confess I only half believed the stories. Diving to the bottom, an otter would return to the surface with a water-rounded stone. Some of the stones we saw were a bit smaller than hen's eggs and roughly the same shape, while others were larger and ranged from more or less spherical to rather flattened ones. Resting the stone on its chest, the otter would hold the mussel between its forepaws, one end in each paw, and strike it smartly a number of times against the stone until the shell cracked. After eating some of the meat the otter would often hammer what was left of the shell on the stone again before resuming its meal. The sound of the hammering was clearly audible, and as charged with magic as if it were the tapping of a genuine leprechaun. One male frequently crammed his mussel back into the corner of his jaws, presumably using his powerful jaw musculature to further fragment the shell. Otters often roll over in the water—my guess is that this may involve some sort of watch for predators, for their only natural enemies are subsurface ones— while they are engaged in a variety of activities. Otters with stones rolled over too, but never lost a stone. While hammering mussels on their stones the otters sometimes held their heads pointing upward, and sometimes stretched their heads forward, chin up. Most of the cubs we saw were nearly full-grown, but were treated with tolerance by their mothers. We saw one cub dive and return with a mussel, but most often the cub simply pestered its parent, poking about the mother's head and chest until it could grasp a morsel. I never saw a mother give food to its young voluntarily, but Jack saw a female tear off bits of mussel in her teeth and turn her head toward her cub, which then took the piece.

We saw only one small cub, which its mother clasped tightly to her chest; most of the cubs were already large, but even these clambered up on their mothers' chests. Reliable eyewitness accounts fit together, however, to provide a most engaging picture of maternal behavior. After a long gestation, presumed to last eight or nine months, the female produces a single cub which, like a guinea pig infant, is well developed, fully furred, and possessed of almost a full set of milk teeth. Its light-cinnamon pelage is thick and long, and extremely buoyant; a small cub I once saw in some motion-picture footage seemed to float almost on top of the water. The cub may be born either on shore or in the water, and it spends much of its early life on the mother's chest, being licked and fondled. The Russian zoologist Barabash-Nikiforov describes a particularly touching scene of a female holding her cub on her chest, sometimes hugging it, sometimes lifting it into the air, turning it over from one side to the other and licking it; he likened the mother's behavior to that of a human being's. In time of danger the female dives, clasping her cub to her self, but when diving for food she leaves it bobbing safely on the surface. The cub stays with its mother for a long period, even, as noted before, when it is nearly as large as its dam, and cubs have been seen with their mothers even after the birth of another baby.

We saw cubs and mothers drift slowly apart as they fed but usually when they were separated by about two hundred feet the cub would swim rapidly back to its mother. Once we saw a cub, thus separated, lose sight of its mother and heard it utter a loud, high-pitched "Waaah!" Just as darkness was falling one evening, two females, each with a cub, fed and dozed in the cove. A large male entered the cove and spent some time visiting with each pair of otters. The females accepted his obviously friendly interest.

To return for a moment to the subject of sea lions and sea otters, we saw numerous instances of both the Stellers and the smaller California sea lions swimming within a few yards—once within about six feet—of otters, without seeming to evoke any interest at all.

Perhaps more important than any other feature of our short stay with the sea otters was the comparative data it added to my own study of the river otters. On first view the sea otter gives one the impression of being a most atypical kind of otter—as it is, in many respects. Still, for all its uniqueness, the sea otter's close kinship to the fresh-water species—particularly the clawless otters—is evident when one has seen at first hand the activities of both. In the five species of river otters that have lived at home with me I had witnessed, without knowing it, actions that have reached their fullest expression in the sea otter. Naturally the river otters spend most of their time right side up, but they do on occasion float briefly on their backs, and of course lie on their backs on land quite often. Frequently, while supine either on land or in the water, my river otters would juggle some small object on their chests—a bottle cap, peanut, or even a pebble. This is a form of play for the river otter, but such play is almost surely the matrix from which the sea otter's use of stones as tools has developed. Again, the river otter's sociability and the sea otter's gregariousness differ more in degree than in kind. This is not to say that any of the present-day species of river otter is the ancestor of the sea otter, but their common ancestor was without question a landlubber, a river-frequenting otter whose behavioral traits diverged in the two main branches of the family tree—keeping within the new patterns the unmistakable signs of their common origin.

*   *   *

Even if I had not had a psychological need to insulate myself from Beever's death and the knowledge that I had brought it about, the spell of the sea otters would have kept me in a state of willing captivity indefinitely. But Jack began to suffer an itch to return home to his wife and unborn baby, so we left for home on a course without further detours.

After my return I drove to the Wisbeskis' and retrieved Beever's corpse, wrapped in a plastic sack, from their freezer. The sentimental may think harshly of me for depositing what was left of my otter in the study collection of the American Museum of Natural History instead of burying his remains in my yard or by some wooded stream but, apart from the scientific data he has yielded, Beever has achieved a form of immortality I will not, for his bones and his pelt will be guarded jealously from destruction as long as the Museum stands.

And Beever left another legacy in death. The autopsy performed on him by the Wisbeskis' veterinarian proved the disease to have been feline enteritis—to my knowledge, the first conclusive indication that the virus affects otters. Treatment based on that knowledge apparently saved Okee, who had become infected from Beever, and after vaccination none of the many otters I now know about have suffered the disease.

Through the remainder of the summer, life gradually returned to normal. Perhaps, I thought, I should remove from the house all traces of Beever's occupancy, yet the gesture would have been a futile one; I knew he had become an indelible part of my life, and I knew too that I would someday bring home another otter. The long cross-country trip had kept me busy with new sights and situations and Jack's companionship. At home, where life was routine again, at least after Zoo hours, I had to struggle continually against the realization of how much Beever's interruptions had become part of the routine. Without them I found it difficult to concentrate.

I was reminded of Beever often. Sometimes the house's sounds at night would snap me out of a half-sleep thinking, and not quite simultaneously knowing the thought to be false, that he was still there. Or I'd see the cement block that I had placed against an air register to keep it from being pulled away. Or the bar across the toilet seat. So many times, too, my thoughts returned to him when no tangible reminder was there. Beever was a good animal, for all his sins against tranquillity.

In mid-September, just before I left to attend a meeting in Washington, D.C., Mary Mitchell lent me an annotated edition of Lewis Carroll's *The Hunting of the Snark*. I had never read it before, and I was unprepared for the stanza that leaped at me from the page, bringing with it a cold resurgence of the grief that had for weeks been mercifully quiescent. Within this masterpiece of buffoonery I found the otter's epitaph:

> But at length he explained, in a tremulous tone,
>   There was only one Beaver on board;
> And that was a tame one he had of his own,
>   Whose death would be deeply deplored.

10   And When She Was Bad . . .

At the fall meeting of the American Association of Zoological Parks and Aquariums in Washington, D.C., I chanced to remark to one of the animal dealers attending that I might be interested in purchasing a tame otter cub if ever one fell into his hands. It just happened, he replied, with a hint of a smile, that he had one at his place in Virginia about fifty miles away. He had tried to make a house pet out of her, but had given up because her odor had begun to permeate the house—she was otherwise in perfect health and docile. The next afternoon I drove out to his home, and not long afterward he arrived from his warehouse with the cub, a half-grown female from Peru belonging to the nominal species *Lutra enudris*, very like Beever except that the naked nose-patch was separated into two small areas around the nostrils, with a haired area between. She was older than I had hoped, but very well behaved. Moreover, she had associated in the house with four little girls of varying ages, a dog and a cat, and was friendly toward strangers (or at least toward me). Within a very few minutes I found myself captivated by everything about her except her name, which was Toodles. She did not look like a Toodles, so on the drive homeward I occupied myself in ruminating over names appropriate for a female otter, and in the end chose Mimsy. The otter, strangely enough, chose to sleep quietly all the way home.

Naming animals has always held an element of travail for me. I had accepted Joey's name only after a long fruitless search for something better; Goop looked like a goop, and I adopted the name when others proved not to fit. Beever's name came in one of those flashes of rare inspiration that just happened, after days of trying on the names of all the Roman and Greek water deities I could find and finding that none were appropriate. The best of them, Poseidon, had a fine ring to it but I knew it would shorten with familiarity to "Posy," and I was damned if I would hang such a name on a male. I was seated on the sofa hand-wrestling the cub and listening to the radio, when I heard a song called "Eager Beaver," from the Richard Rodgers musical *No Strings*. There was a line in the lyrics about a beaver "with teeth so white", and my zoologist's mind rebelled, because the externally visible teeth of a beaver, its incisors, are not white but deep orange; in the next instant my attention was wrenched back to my hand which was being painfully pressed between a set of gleaming white teeth, all too eagerly applied to their task. So the cub became "Beaver," and then because of the inevitable confusion that would arise in my technical notebook I changed the spelling. I was still under the renewed spell of Lewis Carroll when Mimsy came along and, compared to husky Beever, she did look sort of miserable and flimsy.

Almost from the beginning I knew that Mimsy was going to be different. In the essentials of otter behavior she was, allowing for her sex, typical enough, but her personality was hers alone, and at times I have felt that I possessed inside knowledge of why otter females are called bitches.

When Beever died his traveling crate had been with him at the Wisbeskis', and because it was a possible source of infection I left it there with Okee, whose survival provided him with an immunity. Mim had come home with me in a crude wooden crate that I had to destroy to open, so one of my first acts after we got home was to buy a new crate of the type that Beever had had. The first time after I locked Mimsy in it to test her patience I barely reached the door before I heard footfalls pattering behind me. The second time I stayed to watch as she stepped, with almost no squeezing, through the 5 by 1½-inch space between the bars. She grew a little after that and eventually I was able to confine her in the crate, but for the time being I decided to use a cage with one-inch-square openings. The one I had used for Tinca, actually a rectangular incinerator basket, I was equally unwilling to bring home, and had left it at the Zoo to be used for animals not susceptible to feline enteritis. A new one was anything but easy to acquire, but the fourth hardware store I tried had one. I should mention that Mimsy was smaller for her stage of development than Beever had been and never quite attained his size. Whether this was a sexual or a racial phenomenon I do not yet know.

Two days after her arrival I took Mim, in her incinerator, up to my parents' summer home in Sussex County. For a while she behaved admirably. Her own cubhood association with a family of little girls made her confident in the presence of my two nephews. She took the blows of six-months-old Bobby in stride, and he was too young to appreciate the potential danger of retaliation. Richie, four years old, had never seen an otter and was initially afraid of her. He would approach her timidly from behind and, as she turned to look at him, would run wildly away. With her young otter's attraction to moving feet, Mimsy quite naturally took off in hot pursuit. After a while Richie realized that the chase was a game and deliberately lured her into pursuit. As his fear dissipated he eventually held still long enough to wrestle the little otter, and Mimsy kept her nips soft enough that he never complained. Later he brought out his favorite toy, a large pedal-operated fire engine. Mimsy eyed the contraption with alert distrust, and when Richie drove it in her direction terror seized her; for a long time after the boy abandoned the truck Mim avoided its vicinity assiduously, although she continued to frolic with him. Two hours of rough-and-tumble and reciprocating chases tired the cub, and when I brought her into the house she retired under a sofa and slept soundly. Until it was time to leave she was a veritable angel. Then we had our first misunderstanding.

At departure time late that evening, I grasped Mim very matter-of-factly and lifted her in my arms. Like any self-respecting otter she wriggled to free herself and as a result she dropped to the floor from the level of my waist, striking her head. Beever would have yelped and let it go at that, but Mimsy was a half-grown otter and had been with me only a few days, so she did what the situation seemed to call for. To her mind I had been the cause of her hurt. She turned without any growl of warning and bit at my foot five or six times (after the first one or two bites I had the presence of mind to tip up my toe, letting the empty tip of the shoe take the brunt of the attack). Actually her teeth didn't pierce the shoe, something I am certain now she could have accomplished had she really meant me harm. Yet the movements of her head, with arched neck, were snakelike, and I came in time to think of this characteristic action as her "punishing" bite. I thought I knew the otter mind at the time and I had no intention of allowing such an attack upon my person to go unreprimanded, so when she stopped biting I reached down and swatted her. Again, unlike Beever who reacted to a swat with evident chagrin, Mimsy responded by a renewed attack, and I realized that if a truce was to be negotiated I was the one who had to give way this time. A few minutes later she seemed to have forgotten the incident completely. Over the next few months a number of similar incidents occurred, when Mim would slip from my lap or I would step inadvertently on her tail, but over this period of time her response to such real or fancied indignities underwent a gratifying metamorphosis. The first few incidents provoked instant retaliation from her (I knew better than to swat her, though), but in time the attack would be preceded by a pause as she arched her neck in readiness; then she would strike, but with her mouth closed. In the next stage Mimsy assumed the poised position but did not strike, and I cannot escape the conviction that with whatever thought processes existed in her mind, she was, in truth, weighing the situation—she had never been punished for an attack after that first time, so fear of being hit could not account for it. I can explain her ultimate lack of retaliation only by postulating a growing affection for me. At last she abandoned even the preparation for a strike, until if I hurt her she merely yelped and let the matter drop. She had no compunction about biting anyone else who offended her dignity, however, and I had to warn my visitors to watch their feet.

Even from the very first Mimsy's bites, when I was their target, were restrained and never broke my skin. Others, Luke Wisbeski in particular, were not so fortunate. Mim developed an active hatred for Luke to the point of attacking him on recognition. That she had never exerted her full biting strength on me was proved by the way she once punctured a heavy, double-layered leather animal-handler's glove that Luke was wearing during an attempt to regain her trust.

Mimsy's enmity for Luke grew out of two mistakes that she made. In mid-November I took a day off from work and motored to Bound Brook, where I had promised Dotty I would give a talk in the library to the local schoolchildren. Ordinarily I would have left the otter home while away on such a short trip, but the Wisbeskis insisted that I bring her along. They had been over to visit a week before, when Mim was on her best behavior, and they had been impressed with her—I think too that they had decided not to let me make a hermit out of her as I had done with Beever. I left for the library with Dotty thinking vaguely that Mimsy would stay at the Wisbeski home, but Luke had other plans. Slipping a harness on her he took her in his car to the center of town, where he intended to walk her on a lead to accustom her to people, as he had done with Okee. An unkind fate sent a heavy truck past the parked car just as Luke was preparing to attach the lead, and the sight and sound of this monster frightened the otter. She bolted for the window and Luke, knowing how difficult it would be to recapture her on the street in her panic-stricken state, with the added danger that she might dash out in front of a moving car, grabbed at her and held fast. Mimsy evidently did not distinguish this grasp as separate from the appearance of the truck; she whipped around and slashed at his arm, tearing not only his skin but muscle as well. Luke held on and eventually calmed her down, but that was the end of that attempt to urbanize the otter.

By the time Dotty and I were home again Mimsy and Luke

were behaving as if nothing had happened. Luke did mention later, though, that after their return Mim had hidden back of the toilet and growled at his approach, a growl he described as identical to the one Beever used to accord him. From that day on, although Mimsy was as cordial as ever to Dotty, she attacked Luke at every opportunity (once after a separation of seven months). As we attempted to understand this antagonism Luke remembered an incident from their first meeting at our home. Their friend, Art Doering, was with them, and as they were leaving Art accidentally stepped heavily on her tail. Luke was standing close by, and as Mim whipped around the first foot she saw was Luke's. I hadn't witnessed this, and Luke had not thought it important enough to mention at the time. Apparently Mimsy had, in a sense, put Luke on probation after that first hurt, and when he held onto her in the car in Bound Brook he had, in her eyes, overstepped the bounds of friendly behavior.

On the sixth of January we paid our first visit to the Wisbeskis since the automobile incident. Luke was away when we got there, and when he arrived Mim treated him with caution and suspicion, inching close enough to sniff briefly at his shoe, then retreating. By this time I had purchased a pair of heavy animal-handler's gauntlets, made of two layers of tough elk hide. I used them for playing with her because her canine teeth, slenderer and sharper than Beever's, were steadily etching my hands and forearms with a network of shallow scratches and nicks. (I later found a successful means of vocally causing Mim to soften her bite, by uttering an approximation of her own cry of pain, which she understood innately, and the gloves fell into disuse.) A girl who otter-sits for my friends was paying them a visit and with the gloves on engaged Mimsy in a violent but amicable game. Later Luke attempted once more to make up with my otter but when he extended his hand toward her she began to growl in Beever's pitch and timbre. Luke again admitted defeat. Six days later Luke and Dotty paid us a visit, and for the first hour Mimsy played a little with Dotty and, to a much lesser extent, with Luke. After an hour Mim began to growl at Luke with no evident provocation. I was concerned, but I was also thinking like a scientist, and with Luke's approval I set up the tape recorder. I was able to record not only Mim's growl but also the shrill frenzied pitch it rose to just as she struck murderously, with the characteristic explosive snort that accompanies an impassioned attack in many species. It was the kind of display I could never set up deliberately, and I was grateful to my friend for not asking me to lock Mimsy up forthwith. Luke was sitting on the sofa and Mim, lurking under it, darted forward as he prudently raised his feet. She lunged at his heel again and again, snarling and snorting, leaving deep punctures in the rubber of his heel. Dotty, sitting next to him, was ignored.

On another attempt at peacemaking in South Bound Brook, Mimsy lacerated the fingers of my heavy gloves which, happily, Luke extended toward her with his own fingers balled against his palm. On that occasion I had left Mimsy at the Wisbeskis' to drive down to Washington in order to pick up a pair of leopard cubs for the Zoo. In my absence Mim was quartered in the bathroom, where Dotty could stay with impunity. Luke, on the other hand, was exiled and forced to use the extra toilet in the cellar, foregoing showers for the duration of my absence. For the first time, too, Okee was allowed to come upstairs and the two otters met olfactorily, then tactilely, via the space under the bathroom door. The first few times Okee slid his forepaw under the door Mim nipped it, Dotty said, but later he did it unmolested. Okee and Mimsy never met face to face; I would have liked to see if the two (which I doubt were separate species) could interbreed, but Okee weighed at least three times what Mimsy did. Male otters are normally a bit larger and heavier than females; Beever, at fifteen pounds and Mim at twelve would have been properly matched, but Okee at some thirty-odd pounds was just too much otter for such a small female.

We tried once more at the end of February, when I attended the midwinter meetings of the AAZPA in Cincinnati. Again Luke found himself *persona non grata* in Mim's eyes. She refused her canned food on the first day and Dotty began to feed her Okee's beef mixture; thereafter Mimsy rarely accepted the canned food, with the consequence that from that time on any thought of taking her on an extended journey was out of the question. It was the way she greeted me upon my return that really bothered me—rather, I ought to say the way she did not greet me. After a week's absence I expected a contented nuzzling from her, if not an effusive welcome, but she behaved with the reserve she showed to strangers. She was friendly enough, as she always was with a newcomer, but over a quarter of an hour passed before she was sinking her fangs into my flesh just short of puncture, her old playing habit. Then, as I sat on a sofa she straddled my hand and very deliberately covered it with a thin, musky fluid and turned immediately to sniff at it intently.

John Pierrepont, a trustee of the Zoological Society, invited me in May to visit his farm with Mimsy. A little over a year before I had accepted a similar invitation with Beever, who by all odds should have damped Mr. Pierrepont's enthusiasm for otters by the end of that precarious afternoon. It had been a

Sunday in March, when the air was just beginning to take on a tentative warmth.

Beever, safely leashed, had greeted our host with a growl and bitten his shoe angrily; the luncheon that followed was an unorthodox one. Beever, with his leash snubbed around a leg of my chair, growled his warning to Mr. Pierrepont and to the maid who served us. We found it impractical for the maid to serve me because Beever lunged at her feet whenever she drew near, and she had to avoid our vicinity, bringing the food to our host who filled my plate and passed it across the table. With one hand occupied in holding the leash and one eye cocked to watch that Beever's limited movements did not entangle him I muddled my way through lunch, pulling the otter up short when I had to raise the leash hand for such maneuvers as cutting the meat, shifting the leash from one hand to the other as needed. I do not believe that the otter made a good impression on the Pierreponts that day.

On the second visit things went somewhat more smoothly and provided me with some welcome new observations into otter psychology. Mim encountered her first full-sized swimming pool. It was a warm Sunday in late May, and by the time we were ready to set out from home the temperature had already surged into the high eighties. Mim reluctantly permitted me to get her into her travel cage, which I had supplied with several very damp towels to cool her, and I loaded her into the VW along with a refrigerated container of her food and a bottle of Kaopectate as a precaution.

At the Pierrepont farm she behaved amiably toward the members of the family, including Sandy, their Norwich terrier. Sandy was not the first dog Mim had ever seen, but he was not at all shaped like the dogs she had known. Sandy had never seen an otter before, and as a result both animals let curiosity overcome their reserve; in moments a reciprocating chase was under way. I had not been able to strap Mimsy's harness on her beforehand, so when at last Sandy gave her a nip he was banished to the house. I doubt that trouble would have come on the heels of a few more nips, but because I had no way of restraining Mim if it did, the separation seemed prudent. Nearby there sprawled an enormous pasture of tall grass, which was not really the best sort of place to hunt for a frightened otter.

Without the distraction of Sandy's presence, Mimsy very naturally set out to explore the terrace in earnest. Like most other carnivores, otters are intensely curious. In nature curiosity does not kill the cat except on the rarest of occasions, and the animal with this trait more often than not reaps the reward of a richer life. This time the pot of gold at the end of Mimsy's rainbow lay waiting in the guise of an octagonal pool, about four feet in diameter, set at one end of the terrace. She plunged her head into the water but, in the typical response of a "bathtub" otter discovering a deep pool for the first time, she began to feel for the bottom with a paw, unwilling to try water over her depth. At length, however, she did plunge in and found the water to be only about a foot deep. In the pool she found two new conditions: the water was deep enough for her to move in a vertical plane, and the roughly circular shape of the pool allowed her to spin endlessly about the perimeter. In the course of her frolicking she discovered another new treasure, the resident goldfish. At first it was probably no more to her than a fascinating animated toy, differing from the playthings she had in the bathtub at home only in its automatic mobility. Several times she flipped the fish dexterously up onto the flagstones, and each time I plunked it back into the water. Then, just as we decided that we had better rescue the fish and set out to find a temporary container, Mim raised her head out of the water with

L

the fish's tail dangling from the side of her mouth. She tore around the pool again for some minutes in this fashion before hauling up and eating the now very dead creature. Her swim had gone on for about half an hour (with frequent sorties for a reassuring sniff at my shoes) until lunch was served. To avoid

complications I locked her in her travel cage during the meal, even though I knew she would not repeat Beever's performance.

Lunch without Mimsy was delightful and uncomplicated. Afterward I donned a pair of trunks and met the Pierreponts at their swimming pool. By this time five-year-old Jay had joined the family and was splashing in the pool and Mimsy, alarmed by the sight, would not draw nearer until the boy stopped. Then she went through her deep-water reaction again at the pool's edge, leaning down into the water as far as she could stretch while keeping her hind feet firmly planted on the rim. Despite their innate fascination for and love of water, otters are never reckless about it. As cubs they will splash about in the shallows but they must be urged into water over their depth by the mother. Beever's panic in the National Zoo when, after a life as a bathtub otter, he slid into a "bottomless" tank illustrated the point well (although the rapidity with which he adapted to deep water was remarkable).

Mim obviously wanted to partake of the pool but, unlike Beever, made no error in judgment. Eventually I went to the shallow end, walked down the five submerged steps and swam over to her, speaking words and tones of encouragement. She stiffened in alarm and even retreated a little. She was confronted by my usual voice and possibly some scent, but visually I was at that moment just a disembodied head, for from Mim's angle of view the water's surface must have been all reflection. Chimpanzees are known to react with fright to severed heads (in the case reported it was a life-sized anatomical manikin, not a real head) but I had not expected such a reaction from a nonprimate. Nevertheless she relaxed perceptibly when, after I returned to the shallow end, my body emerged gradually into view. With much coaxing I lured her over to where she could reach down and touch the first step, whereupon she slid into the water and explored the tread. Then she hauled herself out. A few minutes later she entered the water again, swimming above the first step with more assurance, until she discovered that the edge led to another step via a shallow drop, and step by step she worked her way very slowly to the bottom. Once she had reached the bottom she was the picture of confidence, and well she might be, having re-enacted an age-old ritual of natural caution. Someone once described an animal (a ferret) as "sauntering along with its hands in its pockets." This sort of exaggerated metaphor describes exactly what an animal does *not* do in a strange situation. Almost invariably it takes a step forward, then another back to safety, then two steps out and two back, always retracing the route to safety against the possibility that the need for a dash toward cover will arise.

In the water Mimsy proved to be a thoroughly unexpected delight as a companion. I was prepared for the rough sport I have seen otters carry out together while swimming, and her violent play on land, I thought, would extend to this new environment. Instead she paddled and dived, porpoised and pirouetted with a grace that took me unawares. And far from trying to twist off my hand, shark-fashion, or clambering up on my head and shoulders using her sharp claws, Mimsy contented herself with approaching me underwater and pushing off again with only the merest brush of her soft palms. When Mr. Pierrepont joined us she treated him in the same delicate fashion, but young Jay's less restrained aquatic locomotion was a bit more than she cared to involve herself with.

Once the little otter had had time to acquaint herself with the pool, I lured her out and away from the water and then ran for the pool, with Mim at my heels, entering it in a flat dive. When I surfaced, Mim was no longer in sight at the edge, but as I turned to see where she would surface Mr. Pierrepont pointed to her head timidly poking out from under the privet, where she had fled upon witnessing my turbulent disappearance. Once again a gradual introduction to a new situation seemed to be in order, so I executed a series of dives from the steps, beginning with one standing in hip-deep water and working my way up the steps until she no longer bolted at the splash. Before long she was nonchalantly diving in at my heels from the edge of the pool.

Most of the time Mimsy swam in what might be described as the Classical Otter Manner, that is, with sinuous twistings, using her hind feet as the principal source of propulsion, with her forelimbs flattened along her chest except for steering or an occasional burst of speed. On the surface, though, she performed a dog-paddle almost but not quite as ungainly as any dog's. At the bottom of the pool she sometimes seemed to be walking, the way hippopotamuses do.

An otter possesses two gifts that enhance its effectiveness in games with a terrestrial companion. The first is the otter's knack for taking shortcuts to head off its moving target—Beever inevitably caught his fox. The second gift is the otter's affinity for water, and Mimsy combined the two to admirable effect when she began to romp with Jay. Both were on land when the boy broke into a dash around the perimeter of the pool with Mimsy in pursuit. But as Jay turned a corner of the rectangular pool Mim slid effortlessly into the water a yard or so from the corner, swam the hypotenuse, and just as effortlessly hauled out practically at his heels.

On our second visit to a large pool, in September, Mim repeated her reluctance at the brink, but the interval of time between her discovery of the steps and her taking to the water was almost negligible. This time we were in Connecticut, where Russ Kinne, the wildlife photographer, had arranged to use a neighbor's pool so we could take underwater pictures of the otter (most underwater shots are taken in small tanks whose boundaries are reflected in the otters' posture, even when not actually visible). The Kinnes did a thorough job of it, with

Russ snapping away underwater and his wife Jane with a camera at poolside, recording Mimsy's actions at the surface. This time I wore a face mask—Mim was not at all upset by the apparition, perhaps because I had let her see me donning it—and the clear vision it afforded me enhanced the magic of her aquatic slitherings.

Although Mimsy looked the picture of health during her session in the pool, a couple of hours earlier near-disaster had struck her. She had been her usual quiet self on the ride to New Canaan, and upon our arrival promptly took over the Kinne home. Whatever qualms I had about letting her fraternize with two-year-old Casey Kinne evaporated when I saw them together. Casey, a tiny, saucer-eyed doll of a girl, properly identified her as an "ot-ter" and comported herself like a child who has socialized with animals before. She made none of the sudden, unpredictable movements common to youngsters, and accepted Mim's investigations calmly, responding in kind. Mim was equally gentle in her response. After a few minutes, just when everything seemed fine, Mim waddled to a corner of the kitchen and defecated. My apologies for her lack of grace died in my throat as I approached the scene of the crime, where even in the dim light the liquid's blood-red color was obvious. Over the next half-hour she had several more movements, all bloody, but unaccompanied by vomiting. In my car I had Kaopectate and a rubber ear-syringe, but Russ instantly produced both items from his own medicine cabinet, and I used them instead. Mimsy recovered rapidly, but left the kitchen splattered with white by-products of her reluctant acceptance of the treatment. The Kinnes, bless them, took everything in stride but, although I cleaned up as much of the mess as I could find, Jane has, I am sure, been confronted since by little white spots. The cause of Mimsy's enteric hemorrhaging remains a mystery, but almost certainly the prompt treatment kept it from becoming a serious condition.

One of the rewards of bringing an animal home that is lacking in field studies of most species is the opportunity for close observation it affords. To my knowledge no information exists concerning the breeding habits of otters in the American tropics other than that a few museum specimens are known to have been pregnant when taken at different times of the year, and that cubs turn up in the hands of animal dealers in all seasons. Common sense would indicate that a tropical species can raise young at any season, but hard data are lacking. Mimsy has supplied part of the answer, at my expense, and in her own way. Since April of 1964 she has come into heat regularly every four and a half to five weeks, after an irregular cycle during the four previous months. Because she was always at hand and easy to examine, it was no problem to see the gradual swelling of her vulva at the onset of her period, but there were other indications as well. For one thing she made a point, very deliberately, of urinating on the sofa (which, through subliminal clairvoyance or dumb luck, I had had re-covered in impervious vinyl). A bit more disconcerting was her tendency to make amorous overtures to me as I lay sleeping. I have alluded earlier to the depth of my slumber—whether it is not impervious to the seductions of a bitch otter or whether I remember only those that took place as I was awakening naturally, I don't know, but the description of Mim's behavior as "amorous" is made from my understanding (such as it is) of the otter viewpoint, most definitely not from my own. To be awakened by a hideous yarling growl with sharp teeth gouging at the calf of one's leg is not my idea of good clean sex. A well-aimed swat seemed to break the romantic spell, though, so my virtue remained intact.

Mimsy's periods of heat, as indicated by the state of her vulva, lasted for about two and a half weeks, with an interval of about two weeks of quiescence, in marked contrast to the somewhat longer heat period of the North American otter, which takes place normally only once in the year.

11 The Doubtful Guest

Toward the end of the summer of 1964 I was routinely scanning a new price list from an animal dealer in Florida when my attention was arrested by a particularly interesting item—naturally enough, an otter. What caught my eye was that the common name "spot-necked otter" was accompanied by the Latin designation of the clawless otter. Both species are African and neither is normally offered for sale in this country—in fact I had never seen a spot-necked otter on any list. So I placed a call to Florida, primarily to assuage my curiosity, and the dealer described the cub to me in enough detail to satisfy me that it was indeed a spot-neck. I should have written rather than phoned, because I found myself asking if the cub was a tame one, and then how much he wanted for it. It looked as if fortune were smiling on me when the dealer was unable to set a price because his African supplier had not yet billed him, and that was that. For the moment I was safe. In spite of my eagerness to see a spot-necked otter, time worked its calming magic and eventually I forgot the matter.

At the end of another call, in September, the dealer reminded me about the otter, named a price that was steep but fair, considering the rarity of the species, and I committed myself after making certain that the animal was in good health and had not recently been near any sick cats or otters. I didn't by any means fall all over myself in my eagerness to acquire this otter, but then neither did I put up a very good fight about it. A few days later the dealer called me to say that the otter was on her way and to add, so very casually, "You remember I said she was tame? Well she *is*—for an otter."

"What does *that* mean?"

"Well, she's very friendly. As long as you don't try to pick her up."

This time I was determined not to risk the life of Mimsy by exposing her to another otter whose health was to be suspect until proved otherwise. I had arranged with the Zoo veterinarian to quarantine the spot-neck for a month in the Animal Hospital before I took it home, and the cub was put into a cage there upon arrival. The cub as it turned out was unquestionably, although not obviously, a male. Young otters are easy enough to sex, after you've seen a few, but until you have they often pose a problem. I named him Samaki, Swahili for "fish," a name that for a long time would seem to be horribly ironic.

Sam went to the Animal Hospital where he was quartered in a four-foot-square cage, restrained unceremoniously, and given the first two of his vaccinations. He ignored the large pan of water, except to drink from it, and spent most of his time trying to make himself as inconspicuous as possible. Inside a small cage is no place to win an otter's trust but there was no other alternative to keeping him there, or so I thought. Then Mary Mitchell contrived to happen along to inspect my new otter, and true to form whipped up a new alternative out of thin air. Poor little Sam, she said, wasn't sick after all, and serving out his quarantine in her home would be far better for him than to endure the impersonal atmosphere of the hospital. I knew that Mary was right, so I protested as faintly as I could, warning her of the not inconsiderable inconvenience that having him would entail. She was adamant, as I knew she would be, and I capitulated, as she knew I would.

None of us really had any idea of what the weeks ahead held in store—not Mary, not Sam, not even I—and that was fortunate.

Mary Mitchell combines the best and the worst features of Auntie Mame, Xantippe and a fairy godmother who has somehow lost the book of operating instructions that came with her magic wand. If she had any reasonably normal friends she managed over the years to keep them out of view, in spite of my sometimes unannounced visits. Instead, an impromptu descent upon the Mitchell household would likely involve meeting a lady who dozes off halfway through her second whisky sour and begins to snore softly. It was less likely (but once was more than enough) to produce the unnerving confrontation with a strange, tipsy woman who sauntered up to me and to Mary's surprise and my horror clutched me suddenly in a passionate embrace from which my disentanglement was somewhat less than graceful. After a while I learned to approach the house warily and to take almost anything in stride.

The rest of the household comprised two aging castrated tomcats, Timmy, a slightly aloof but placid gray and white cat, and his nemesis Toby, a baleful white tyrant with one green and one blue eye. Timmy never more than rubbed across my ankles, but Toby, whenever I wore a suit that promised to show white cat-hairs to the best advantage, would leap into my lap and lean upright against my chest. On special occasions he would slyly rest both soft paws against my neck and, after biding his time, unsheath his claws ever so gently, usually when I had something undroppable in each hand. I do not understand cats.

Mary's husband Ash was the oasis of normalcy in the place. Upon him fell the burden of foreseeing the complications that would arise from keeping a tiger cub or an orphaned llama at large, but as with most husbands it was always his lot to play the devil's advocate and then be steam-rollered into accepting what must be. I never saw any of the preliminaries to Sam's invasion of the Mitchells', but I can imagine the debate. The otter was taken there from the Zoo after his first vaccine dose and, groggy from the slight reaction that followed, he cowered in his cage for the remainder of the day and all of the first night.

In those first days Sam had about his person a scent so heavy that you felt it might become visible at any moment and hide him from sight. Young *Lutra* otters are characterized by a smell that is malty and slightly musty, and altogether pleasant, even when the absence of swimming has allowed it to intensify. In time these cubs take on an adult smell which, too, is not unpleasant. Because we humans are as a species sight-oriented and little cognizant of the nuances of scent, I have some justification in describing the typical otter scent as somewhat doggy; it will get the point across to anyone who has never experienced the unique otter perfume. Sam, on the other hand, did not have this ottery smell, but had a different one that was rendered almost suffocating in its concentration. Weeks later, after he learned to like water, Sam's aura subsided to a tolerable level, and though it differed from the *Lutra* otter smell, it was in itself not a bad scent.

Mary installed the otter in her bedroom on the second floor, a room not really designed with the human-otter relationship in mind, for its furnishings provided too many crevices large enough to harbor a beast. From Sam's point of view it was eminently suitable, though, and for the same reason. His cage was a metal-bottomed, wire-screened shipping crate some four feet long, with a removable sliding door at one end. The crate rested parallel to and near Mary's bed, not very easy to get to, but visible from the bed. For the first two days Sam refused to leave his sanctuary in the cage; for the remainder of his five-week stay the problem became one of getting him back into the cage for the night. During these attempts to confine him Sam showed a dismaying new facet of his personality, first to Mary and then to me.

Otters are built as snakily as any mammal and, like snakes, they are supple beyond belief. When I was a kid fascinated by herpetology I soon learned how to put a snake into a sack—you had to be thoroughly vigilant lest the head of the cooperative snake, sliding into the bag, exit again while its tail was still on the way in; snakes have a way of doing this. And so did Sam. Good little otter that he was, he meekly suffered himself to be stuffed into his cage, but while his hindquarters were being guided into the cage out would pop his head. So far, it was all a great game, but make any attempt to stop his egress—even with a symbolically outstretched hand—and a viper-quick strike would leave you with four punctures. There was never any malice in these bites, rarely a second bite, and never a gratui-tous twist of the teeth in your flesh; as a matter of fact Sam would have let go and continued his escape even before your consciousness registered the pain of the bite. And immediately, too, Samaki would be his old lovable self. The bites were never severe enough to more than just break the skin, and even this was probably the fault of the flimsiness of human construction, since such a bite would never pierce an otter's hide.

Well, I have to qualify my remark about the force of his bites. On one occasion, one of Sam's canines happened to hit a vein on Mary's wrist where her skin was particularly delicate. Blood spurted from the wound, not in great quantity, but enough to leave a small puddle on the floor before Mary stanched the flow. Sam, who had evidently forgotten the incident already, was mooching around the floor, when he discovered the blood. He sniffed at it intently and proceeded to lap it up; then he turned his eyes upward in the full bloom of innocence to see why Mary was so quiet. Happily for everyone concerned, the old story about the consequences of an animal's first taste of human blood—how it will make him seek it thereafter—is nonsense. Either that, or Sam has since exercised a remarkable control over the blood-lust raging within his savage breast. After these biting incidents it became necessary to cage Sam through guile, and the less said of these contests the better.

Still smelling somewhat beyond high heaven, Samaki, my wriggly Swahili fish, would have no more to do with water than either of the Mitchell cats. He'd slither through the drinking water and through a large, shallow, pottery birdbath Mary put into the cage, but that was his limit. He would rear up to peer over the rim of Mary's bathtub, looking for all the world like Edward Gorey's drawings of the "Doubtful Guest," but peering was all he did.

Mary's bathroom had a shower stall as well as a tub, and she hit on the idea of putting Sam's toys in the stall and allowing him to play with them there unmolested and unmoistened. Then she added a large plastic litter pan half-filled with water. Sam drank heartily. He must have sensed a plot afoot, though, because after this first encounter with the water pan he began to

hesitate about entering the stall, until only the presence of a particularly attractive toy could lure him in—and then he would only slither carefully past the pan, grab the toy, and run.

If water held no special charm for the little otter, it would seem that nearly everything else did in a room furnished with no thought at all of otters. The bureau stood on legs just high enough for a smallish otter to squeeze under and establish himself in an impregnably defensible position for as long as he liked. And Sam did, whenever the fancy took him. Next to the bureau there was a cylindrical metal wastebasket just begging to be overturned and rolled nosily to the bed, under which it would not quite fit, providing thereby endless opportunities for seeing whether it wouldn't *really* fit if it were just tugged or pushed long and loudly enough. An overstuffed chair in one corner soon grew to be understuffed, and because visitors to the room normally sat in it Sam found he could lurk beneath it, undetected behind the chair's hanging skirts, and investigate new feet in secrecy. This was how the otter really satisfied his curiosity about me and I never knew it until, with growing confidence, he pressed his nose to my ankle. After that he indulged in cuff-pulling, and finally in sniffing at the hand I dangled down with carefully affected nonchalance.

In time Sam let me touch him, something he had long since let Mary do, but only after he had bitten her in fright a few times. How often he bit Mary I never found out, because Mary wasn't about to turn informer; I saw two bites take place and caught Mary with fresh puncture marks on a couple of other occasions, but she always brushed off any effort I made to pry deeper into the circumstances by telling me, with a note of irrevocable finality, that it had been her fault.

My visits to see Sam were few and brief, because Mimsy was at home and needed attention. Then in late October, when Sam had been at Mary's three weeks, I felt confident enough to deposit Mimsy at the Wisbeskis' and leave for a zoo conference in Houston, Texas. By the time I returned at the end of the month Mary looked frazzled and eagerly—*almost* eagerly—got Sam ready for his move to my home. He had passed through his quarantine without any trouble. The same could not, unfortunately, be said for the Mitchell household. In my absence Sam had torn out the bottom of Mary's box spring and taken up residence inside. Mary had spent most of the night lying awake, scarcely daring to move for fear of squashing down a spring on some part of Sam's anatomy. Sam was without much doubt sufficiently alert and agile to avoid such an occurrence, so Mary need not have worried. The worst that seems to have happened to the cub was that lint within the box spring set him to sneezing sporadically. The following day Mary called the Zoo and a keeper came over to extract the recluse. They then turned the spring over and Sam's new hideaway was put off bounds.

Thanks to Mary's ingenuity the cub began to develop a more proper relationship with water, too, while I was away. Noticing that he had avoided the plastic pan in the shower stall, but that he did seem to enjoy wallowing in the shallower crockery birdbath in his cage, Mary added the birdbath to the stall, and with this familiar object in view the stall seemed to lose some of its menace. In short order she found him lying with his hindquarters in the birdbath and his head and shoulders in the plastic pan. He looked up at her when she approached, and then went back to what he had been doing, dunking his head and executing half-rolls. Mary found his performance "ridiculous," but comforting in that it was a beginning. Later that day she thought she saw him holding his nose under the water for a few seconds at a time, the critical experiment in breath-holding that seems to mark the end of cubhood and the beginning of an otter's brief novitiate. Mary watched Sam as intently as a hawk perched above a mouse's nest and confirmed her suspicion—Sam had taken the plunge, at least figuratively. In succeeding days he came to spend more time at the pan, keeping his head submerged for longer periods, while he pushed his various floating toys around with his nose; he even deigned to wallow in it. On the other hand, nothing Mary could do would induce him to enter the bathtub.

M

By the day I arrived to deliver Mary from Sam, and Sam to New Jersey, the otter's aquatic world had expanded a little farther. The pan and birdbath were gone from the shower stall and the stall itself formed a shallow pool. Mary had contrived a makeshift plug for the drain and Sam had some three inches of depth to slosh around in. Mary's carpeting was damp some distance from the bathroom, its moisture content increasing with proximity to the bathroom sill. The bathroom itself was also carpeted, and Sam's newfound excesses had made it squishy underfoot. The only thing an otter indulges in in moderation is moderation itself.

12 A House Divided

Home with me, Sam decided to play it safe. In spite of his five weeks as a house otter, during which time he was not mistreated by a long shot (he was spoiled if anything), the otter stayed in the security of his travel case and surveyed the new surroundings. From his arrival in early afternoon until late in the evening, Sam preferred to remain in his case—the same case he had so often steadfastly refused to enter when Mary wanted him to. But when at last the spirit moved him to show himself he was not the cub I had worried about, cringing in a carrying case, afraid of every new sound. In crossing the threshold from the case to his new house he seemed to leave his fear behind, and I had an otter with a full head of steam on my hands. And on my feet, which I had prudently protected with boots.

I had been sitting patiently on the sofa, reading, when I heard the slap-slap of Sam's feet approaching around the corner and under my seat. Slowly I dropped my hand for him to smell, so he'd know who I was. My right hand was dangling with its back presented to him (if you try this on a sofa you'll see that it isn't a comfortable position at best). I didn't realize how awkward it was, though, until Sam took my thumb in his teeth, not at all gently, and tried to yank it under the sofa, perhaps for a closer look. There was no way I could move with him; my arm refused to bend backward and for a time things got sticky until, after a moment of calculation, I figured out what I had to do with the rest of my body to get myself in a position from which I could move with the tug. Simply pulling free was out of the question, for Sam had all four canine teeth pressing against the thumb and would in all likelihood have dug them in if he had felt his hold slipping.

Before long he let go and turned to playing in earnest, roughly enough to make me reinforce my verbal complaints with an occasional clout, and a few times my hand made enough of an impression on him to subdue his high spirits. Otters are not very adept at sulking, so a little coaxing would always bring him back with undiminished enthusiasm, but fortunately with lesser jaw pressure.

Samaki's first twenty-four hours in the house disclosed an entirely new aspect of the destructive capabilities of otters. Things that had never occurred to his predecessors began to happen thick and fast. He found the drawstring for the window draperies and naturally enough tried to pull in the wrong direction, putting his back into the effort; I've shortened it since. He removed all of the cushions from the chairs and sofa, and lacerated two nonremovable cushions. Some weeks later he dismantled a Danish chair, piece by piece, and in the months that followed I found myself disposing of one chair after another. He discovered the plastic litter pan with its contents of wood shavings; this he dumped in one grand movement, spilling, along with the shavings, some of his own stool that I had put there to give him an incentive to use the pan, as Mimsy did. He did a number of other things that day and night, but mercifully I no longer recall them, nor do I care to.

Destruction was to be Sam's hallmark. All that he did that

evening to point out the weaknesses in the otterproofing it had taken me years to devise were but a foretaste of things to come. But things did settle down, a little bit at least, and I could begin to savor the positive side of Sam's unique personality. He is the only otter I have known personally ever to have invented a two-player game. I suppose that the definition could be applied to the wrestling matches that otters indulge in with their owners or other animals, but I have never seen an inanimate object brought into play with a partner, except in an accidental way. Normally, if an otter playing with some small object is approached by a partner, human or otter, he experiences an instant loss of interest in the plaything and gives his full attention to the living partner. Sam, on the other hand, invented a game of "fetch" with me. As with all creatures lutrine, however, the game had to be played according to *his* rules; I could never initiate the game, and it ended when he decided it should. But as often as I tried to get him to associate the word "fetch" with his actions he would have none of my addendum to the rules.

When a game of "fetch" was to be commenced Sam would amble over to me carrying in his mouth or pushing along the floor with nose or paw some toy, a ball, rubber ring, or his nylon bone. Leaving it at my feet the otter would look up expectantly. On the first occasion I suspect I deserved as much credit for intelligence as he did, since I guessed his remarkable intent in the face of all past experience with otters. Still, there is no doubt in my mind that Sam wanted me to throw the ball; the game arose from anything but accident. I threw the ball, musing on this behavior that seemed to be so un-otterlike, and almost before I knew it the ball was back, gently bumping my toe, and there was Sam, gazing up again. The game went on for quite some time, long enough at least for me to tire of it first. But I'm not a bad sort, really, so I kept playing until my mentor decided to call it quits.

One of the more interesting features of our "fetch" sessions was the great difference between Sam's behavior and that of the dogs I've known. The old trick known as "faking out" in sports didn't work on the otter. Almost any dog will begin to run to the spot where he thinks the ball will land as you begin your throw; hold on to the ball and the dog keeps running for a while, until he discovers the trick. And my dogs never seemed to learn to wait. Sam, on the other hand, could never be fooled. He never began his run until the ball was in motion. Otters are said by some to be nearsighted, and this may actually be true, but Sam followed the moving ball unerringly. Movement may be the factor rather than visual acuity, but I have seen otters in the house race across the room where a small moth fluttered near the floor and pursue it relentlessly as it continued its flight at a higher altitude.

While at Mary's Sam had come to enjoy playing with fresh raw peas. Small as they are, raw peas bounce phenomenally and erratically, lending to the chase an air of unpredictability that other inanimate toys lack. He seldom had a chance to encounter a pea now, because no self-respecting bachelor is going to shell and cook his peas when he can get them all done up and frozen in the supermarket, and a frozen pea, even when thawed, has very little bounce. But every so often I would return from dinner at the Mitchells' with a bag of unshelled peas, and Sam would reward Mary's thoughtfulness with the attention it deserved. At first the peas were only miniature toys, but eventually he got around to biting them, liked the taste, and thereafter ate them greedily. In fact the end of his interest in them as toys in later sessions came to be signaled by the sounds of chewing instead of chase, and I'd know that the time had come to return the remaining peas to the refrigerator until the next day. The finely chopped particles of Sam's peas went through his innards undigested. I wasn't overly surprised that he should eat such seemingly unnatural food, because North American otters in the wild are known to glut themselves on wild blueberries in season, but I have since been taken slightly aback when I read in a paper by M. A. E. Mortimer, in *The Puku*, a Rhodesian game journal, that one of the two spot-necks he kept for observation took peas (and beans, potatoes, and carrots) from his garden.

The evening after Sam's arrival I brought Mimsy back from the Wisbeskis'. She took the drive without complaint, and when we got home I let her go directly into the tub for a swim. Although the house was already sufficiently permeated with Sam's scent to affect even my nose Mim seemed to pay it no attention. It may be that she had long since detected Sam's musk in my clothing after my visits at Mary's, and that in the absence of anything significant to associate it with she found it uninteresting. If anything, Mimsy's nonchalance made things a little easier for me because, with her safely in the tub, I had time now to get Samaki locked up in his own crate, and their meeting could be controlled. As pessimistic as ever, and in spite of the past introductions of other otters that had taken place without a hitch, I was determined to leave as little as possible to chance. The reward of such an inflexible attitude is that sooner or later events will justify the position, whatever it is. This time the precaution turned out to be well taken. Sam, as usual, saw to it that his caging was a major undertaking, but at last it was done. Mim went docilely into her cage. Then I pushed the two enclosures together. The menace in Mimsy's growl was unmistakable, and although Sam appeared not to recognize it, I decided to stop the introduction after a few minutes; the hour was late.

The pattern for the weeks that followed was much the same. Sam's activities were restricted to the living room-dinette half of the house and Mimsy's to the rest. When the double-cage meetings failed to improve Mim's attitude I tried to let things happen more spontaneously, and while she sloshed around in the tub I'd give Sam the run of the house. Sam of course wanted nothing better than to share the company of the older animal, so a good part of his time he spent at the doors of the tub enclosure, peering sideways with cocked head through the crack between the doors or pressing his nose against the slit, drinking in the lady's scent. I could tell when he was at the tub doors by the low moaning growl that was Mimsy's acknowledgment of his presence. Sometimes on my return from work I could hear Mim at the door that separated her half of the house from Sam's and, holding my hand at the space beneath it, I would be greeted by her friendly chuckle. By this time Sam would appear, press his nose to the crack, and Mim's voice would change to a growl.

At last I fashioned a high plywood partition that could be wedged into the doorway. In the lower half I cut a foot-square opening covered with wire mesh. Most of the time the only function this device served, other than providing an irritating obstacle over which I had to climb to get into the other rooms, was to give Samaki a view of Mimsy's territory. Mim avoided it obstinately. With a great deal of coaxing I could call her to the screen, but at the first sight of the intruder in her life she would wheel around and dash away.

Toward the end of November I had to make a trip to Washington. Rather than go through the complications of imposing the otters on friends (it would mean two sets of friends this time, because of the one-sided incompatibility that existed) I took the air shuttle down early in the morning and prepared to return in the evening. However, a fog had settled in on the New York area. Newark Airport, where I had left my car, had been closed down completely, and I was just lucky enough to be able to catch a plane bound for La Guardia Airport, located within the confines of New York itself. The helicopter service between the two airports had also been shut down, I was told, so I called my father and asked if he could meet me at La Guardia.

Apparently my plane had just beaten the fog to the airport, because the trip back with Pop was a horror. I'd like to be able to say that had I known how dense the fog was I would not have asked his help; the truth is that I had two hungry otters at home, and I couldn't let them go through the night unfed without risking serious harm. By the time we reached Newark Airport the visibility was down to almost zero. I found the Garden State Parkway more by instinct than by sight and began the long crawl home. I calculated roughly how much distance I had to stop in should another car suddenly appear before me and, based on this, never had the car moving above twenty miles per hour. Far too often other drivers, perhaps assigned to guardian angels with faster reflexes than mine, zipped past me at speeds recklessly high.

At three in the morning, give or take a few minutes, I reached the front door, fully expecting to find a mess, the otter solution to boredom. I did. In fact I found two messes, one in each half of the house. Sam had de-cushioned the sofa, punctured the seat cushion, and removed generous quantities of fiber stuffing from the seat pad and one arm of a very comfortable chair. Mimsy had been content merely to work open the lowest drawer of my dresser and strew out the contents; then, for good measure, to climb up to the top of the dresser and dump off the assortment of debris I had been letting collect there. Things could have been worse.

Mimsy's temperament was undergoing a change that had begun some months earlier. With the regularization of her heat periods she had turned sporadically unmanageable, cranky and messy, depositing a smoky-scented musk on the cushions and, when I wasn't alert, on me. As I noted before, she began to favor me with amorous attacks as I lay sleeping at night. These affronts grew more intense with the passage of time, but I sus-

pect too that the unsettling effect of Sam's presence had something to do with them. Emil Liers, who has spent a lifetime in
concentrated study of the North American otter, has told me
that most of his females became nasty as they came in heat, and
Mimsy was following the pattern perfectly. Ordinarily the
courtship of otters is a noisy, fierce affair with a good deal of
biting on both sides, so I can pass off most of Mim's behavior as
perfectly normal. But she didn't always sleep with me; often for
days at a time she would choose the clothes hamper or the bottom drawer of the dresser, returning to my bed, I recall, on the
colder nights. Sometimes I would be awakened by her staccato
caterwauling, half expecting the sting of her teeth, only to realize the sound came from elsewhere in the room, and a quiet
search would disclose the otter sound asleep. To me no other
explanation, makes sense except to assume that the otter's
sounds are made only under appropriate circumstances, and
that in these instances the circumstances were taking place in a
dream as real to her as mine are to me. As nearly as I can tell,
her most intense nocturnal displays, both in dreams and when I
was their butt, took place following a day on which Mimsy had
reacted with particular violence toward Sam. Her behavior toward the strange cub was of course conditioned in part at least
by her sexual excitement, but I can't help but think that another factor was her previous isolation from otters, and I believe
that even without the complications of physiology she would
have resented the newcomer.

Whatever the explanation that underlay her behavior, that
behavior was hastening the day when Mimsy could no longer be
accorded bedroom privileges. With increasing frequency there
were nights when I would be driven from my warm bed by the
otter, and with a subsequent appearance of disorientation she
would often stay spurred to the attack even after I had removed

myself. These prolongations of hostility had an unreal quality that I am at a loss to describe, except to say that Mimsy seemed not to be in possession of her faculties—in a human we would call it a kind of madness or trance. After a while, as I chuckled to her she would slowly come to her senses and calm down, then follow me meekly to the tub, where I would lock her in for what was left of the night, with a towel or two to sleep on.

The length of time I had to spend chuckling on these occasions is an indication of Mimsy's abnormal state, for this form of friendly communication under normal circumstances would quickly divert her from an incipient state of hostility. By way of illustration let me recount a situation that arose during the same period.

I have already mentioned the otter's new tendency when in heat to mark with musk and urine objects that she had previously left alone. Less consistently, she also defecated in places other than her litter box, and one of the more annoying of these new places was a particularly difficult-to-get-at corner under my bed. An otter is strongly influenced by scent in choosing a spot for elimination, and once a place has been used the temptation is great to use it again. Following such mishaps I clean the area thoroughly until I can no longer detect an odor; the otter's sensitive nose may still find some, so I then use a strong disinfectant. These routine procedures failed in the present case, so I had taken to adding paradichlorobenzene moth crystals to further make the area unpleasant. Evidently Mim returned to the spot for reasons other than scent, held her breath, and performed the forbidden act; and on one of the last of these occasions when I caught her at it I tried the last idea in my repertoire. Instead of speaking meanacingly to her I growled her growl at her, believing that in using her inborn "language" my message would get across more surely. The message reached her so clearly that she growled back, if anything more ominously than I had done, and at that point the only graceful way out left to me was to chuckle to her, as one otter does to another to avoid a brewing fight. It worked, and Mim came over, chuckling in return. I think that if Mim had come to me unweaned, and had formed the offspring-parent relationship that such cubs do, my growl would have carried authority and might have accomplished its objective. But Mimsy, and Sam too, had been half-grown on arrival and my relationship to each was, from their viewpoint, more one of equals, with me having a slightly upper hand, perhaps because I was such an enormous otter. "All animals are equal, but some animals are more equal than others," fortunately.

At length Mimsy's behavior grew to be so unpredictable (unless one made a point of making dire predictions) that getting her up when I arrived home became a problem. She was still permitted to sleep in my bed by day, in spite of my realization that often she would refuse to vacate it even at bedtime. She slept as soundly as the dead, but any attempt on my part to waken her by a touch aroused her to fury. Ordinarily she slept under the lower sheet, but even the taut cloth between us "gave" enough for her snaps to be effective, and a few times she emerged from the bed still ready to do battle. There had to be another way to wake her and bring her forth in a manageable mood. I must say, with justifiable pride, that I found such a way. For want of a better term I named it "the Bert and Harry routine."

Unlike the shy, retiring Sam, Mimsy always had an insatiable curiosity about strangers. Let anyone walk into the house and no matter where she happened to be the new voice would bring her out for a close look. It had to be a new voice—she never reacted this way to my voice when I spoke on the phone. So I began to hold conversations with myself, out of sight of the bed. One side of the dialogue I did in a different voice, the other in my own, and the usual effect would be to draw Mimsy irresistibly out of the bed and out of the bedroom, past me, to search the rest of the house; then I could with no difficulty feed her or lead her to the tub for the night. I suspect that when her response to my ruse failed it was because I had run out of new voices; most likely she came to realize that the old ones never provided real strangers to inspect.

Time seemed to be doing nothing to soothe Mimsy's upset where Sam was concerned, but it was overseeing Sam's development, in some ways to the good and in others to the contrary. He was climbing regularly up onto the long cabinet in front of the large living-room window now, and in the beginning I could find no objection since he seemed mainly to use it for sleeping. But then he started to turn the top into a latrine. My first countermeasure involved setting mousetraps along the perimeter of the top, but in the mornings often I would find traps sprung and other more tangible signs of Sam's visits. The first few times Sam had been smacked on his sensitive nose by the traps, but he learned with unsettling ease to press his neck over both the trigger and the snapper. Thus immobilized, the trap could not snap, and when Sam eased his weight off gradually the snapper would maintain harmless contact with him until, at the critical height, it slammed down clear of him. A trap that had been disarmed in this way, Sam found, made a marvelous toy for juggling or pushing around. Finally, in desperation, I bought a battery-operated shocking device of the kind used to electrify fencing in pastures. It was harmless, but delivered quite a wallop. Again I had underestimated my opponent, and the first arrangement, with copper wire taped to the cabinet top, was unworthy of Sam's intelligence. Forthwith he contrived to tear a wire free and short out the circuit with it. Most of the time this dastardly deed was done in the dead of night, but once or twice he did it almost under my nose. Fortunately I learned to recognize a short in the device (which I came to dub the "Doom Machine" because of the ominous "thunk" it made as it sent out each electrical pulse) from the way it made the TV picture flip. Following this breakthrough I came to recognize the pop on my bedside radio, so I could detect a short even at a distance. The next step was to substitute metal bars for the wiring and screw them fast to the cabinet. Now it worked like a charm. For a while.

The wolverine of the northern reaches of North America and Eurasia has a reputation, well deserved on circumstantial evidence, of being a demon devoted to the destruction of trappers. There are authenticated stories of this large mustelid breaking into a trapper's cabin while the owner was out on his line. The trapper would return from days in the cold to find the inside of the cabin literally shredded—furniture torn apart, cupboards broken open and their contents strewn around. Any of his food that had not been eaten would be fouled beyond use, and like as not the trapper would have to leave the area in defeat, his supplies and sometimes his shelter demolished. The wolverine and the otter are cousins. From this one fact I have developed a theory, and I present it here briefly in the wolverine's defense: what he is alleged to do to trappers' cabins is done not out of malice but in the spirit of exuberant curiosity. Here, as Exhibit A for the defense, is what one otter who bore me not the slightest ill will will accomplish one evening when I failed to return on time.

I had been to the Mitchells', cadging a balanced meal, and what with one thing and another I didn't return until eleven o'clock. At some point after six Sam had begun to realize that I was late (or, to be more scientific, he had probably begun to notice that the usual routine was amiss). I picture him beginning to poke around the place looking idly for amusement. That it was not hunger I am certain, since his evening meal was never given until nearly midnight. The only triggering factor I can perceive is my absence. Most likely he figuratively twiddled his thumbs on and off from about seven until ten. By this time the solitude began to affect him in earnest. At last, some time in the vicinity of ten thirty, Sam could stand it no longer. There had to be *something* to do, and the window cabinets were an inviting place at which to do it.

One of Samaki's preferred pastimes had been to move the heavy base cabinet that stood directly in front of the window, the one I had electrified. The top of this cabinet stood level with the jutting window sill, so that there existed a space perhaps an inch and a half wide between the cabinet and the wall. Give an otter enough space to wedge his nose in between two objects and he can pry apart almost anything that isn't rooted to the spot. When Sam first took up furniture moving I loaded the cabinet with cement blocks and sat back very pleased with myself. He calmly shoved the whole thing away from the wall again. After that I bolted the base cabinet to the wall, and that was that. On either side of the central cabinet (which was five feet long) stood two two-foot-wide chests, and upon each was stacked a two-foot-high, glass-doored case. A broad shelf spanned the cases at their tops, and upon the shelf were two more cabinets, each filled with a variety of small things that are best kept away from an otter. The weight of this complex is enormous.

Sam climbed up on the central cabinet, the one bolted to the wall. He couldn't make a frontal assault because the Doom Machine was working, and a climb from the front would take him across the electrified strips. Because of the windowsill, which extended a few inches behind the short base chests too, the entire assembly stood out from the wall. With my usual clear head I had judged correctly that the combined weight of everything stacked on the small chests would make them too heavy to be moved. But I had overlooked the fact that where there was no window sill Sam might be able to get up unscathed. He did. I overlooked other facts: that (a) the tremendous weight was concentrated on four legs under the base cabinet, providing a high coefficient of friction, that (b) the stacked chests had less than the total weight of the three levels, and that (c) the weight of the upper cabinets was evenly distributed over their lower surfaces, greatly lowering the coefficient of friction. None of this occurred to Samaki; he simply got his nose behind the case in the middle of the stack, wormed his way in behind it until he could use his paws, heaved it away from the wall, out from under the shelf, and left it precariously teetering over the edge of the base cabinet. The end of the shelf kept it from from falling all the way, but in so doing the shelf tipped a little, just enough to allow the uppermost cabinet—which held my camera, bottles of ink, and tubes of paint, among other things—to slide off and drop nearly four feet to the floor, spewing forth its contents. Possibly the top cabinet didn't slide by itself. Sam is an accomplished enough chimneyer to have scrootched up and helped launch it to glory. That part I don't know about, but I am reasonably certain that the result of his little adventure was somewhat more than the otter had bargained for. In my mind I can hear the crash and see Samaki the Terrible leap heedlessly over the electrified metal strips, skid across the floor, and pick himself up, running, probably to his hiding place under the sofa from which he nervously awaited the cabinets' next act of hostility. Not too long after that I arrived, during the period of shock when he hid lest the furniture attack him again. This I

N

assume because I found no evidence that he had gained the courage since this outrage to return to the scene of the crime and discover the veritable Montezuma's hoard of paint tubes, lenses, ink, and of course my Exacta, with its lens-mount now rakishly askew.

As I stood silently assessing the disaster I felt a soft nose touch my ankle and glanced down to see the two shoe-button eyes that alternately cast innocent looks at me and wary ones toward the exploded cabinets. The defense rests.

13 Period of Adjustment

I haven't said anything so far about the operational side of maintaining a divided house with at least one otter who favored abolition of the system. The details are not very interesting, and are such that anyone driven by necessity could work out more or less satisfactorily. Sam, needless to say, was the real challenge, but for a few days I had help of an unexpected sort in getting him to move at times of my choosing.

During Sam's stay with Mary I had traveled to Houston, Texas, to the AAZPA meeting, and had stopped off at several other Texas zoos before returning. The Fort Worth Zoo is small but excellent, and on top of that was the only zoo I'd ever visited that carried souvenirs worth buying. Most zoos, my own included, sell only cheap junk like hats with fluorescent pink ostrich feathers and celluloid airplanes, but Fort Worth (which sells its share of such items) also had a selection of really decent articles. The prize in my selection was a cast stone frog, stylized, very flat and broad, and some fourteen inches long. Sam was elsewhere when I set it down before the fireplace, and when he encountered it for the first time his reaction was one of surprise and great fear. He came loping toward the fireplace, unaware, until, confronted by the frog, he jammed on the brakes, reared up and whirled around, uttering an explosive snort; before this he had once given the same response to a bag of laundry, but

that time he quickly overcame his upset and investigated it thoroughly with nose and paws. The frog was clearly different; for two hours he skulked about "Fff-ing" at it, keeping it in sight, and never approaching nearer to it than ten feet. It affected him, obviously, as more than just another strange object.

By the time two hours of this had passed it dawned on me that the frog could be put to a good use, and I removed it from view. Then for several days, at least, I could herd Sam anywhere I wished just by brandishing it at him. In time, however, the frog's immobility and failure to press an attack gave Sam confidence, and he accepted it as part of the habitat. But while the frog's spell lasted I had an awesome power over him.

The frog reaction disappeared before I had the presence of mind to set up a tape recorder, so I tried to devise a new experiment in order to capture Samaki's vocal responses.

They were, as I've said earlier, very different from Mimsy's,

since Sam was a very different kind of otter from Mim. His color pattern was different—deep, lustrous brown above, scarcely lighter below, in contrast to Mim's lighter, grayer brown that became silvery on the underside; most conspicuous was Sam's hodgepodge of white to yellow spots and blotches on his throat. But these are rather superficial differences. The spot-necked otter was once set aside in its own genus, *Hydrictis*, but lately zoologists have put it back into *Lutra* on the premise that it does not differ significantly from the otters of Eurasia and the

New World. But the spot-neck *is* a different breed of otter. Sam's face has more the look of a marten or weasel than an otter, due principally to the comparatively weak development of his facial whiskers. In consequence of this the fleshy tissue of his muzzle and lips is underdeveloped, and he lacks the broad, catfish look of *Lutra* otters.

Another difference lies in the repertoire of vocal expressions used by each species for communication. Certain of a species' sounds are peculiar to that species, and the "language barrier" it produces between related species occupying the same region is a factor that helps reduce the possibility of hybridizing (and thus "wasting" a mating). Where Mimsy uttered a harsh "Hah!" when in a state of anxiety, Sam's equivalent was a *"Fff!"* sound. Where Mimsy's cry of pain was a sharp *"Ee!"* Sam uttered a birdlike trill. On the other hand, Sam's snort when startled is similar to the one used by all species of otter, and although he has always been too good-natured ever to challenge anyone, his growl is doubtless the one common to all otters. Unfortunately Sam is a very silent animal, and I have not as yet been able to discover his full vocabulary. Several times I have heard a tantalizing bark, most un-otterlike, but he never repeats it when a tape recorder is handy and I have been unable to discover its context.

The *"Fff!"* sound was one I felt sure I could elicit experimentally, so I went out and bought a mechanical monster, a bilious green plastic thing sold under the name "Horrible Harrison." The monster measured about ten inches in length and stood some five inches high, in the form of a misshapen insect with two bulging black, white, and red eyes, and a wicked-looking pair of black pincers. Pulling out a string in its nether region set the monster lurching across the floor to the accompaniment of a loud rasping buzz. On several occasions I confronted both Sam and Mimsy, separately, with the device. Each reacted in the same way, with apprehension of such low intensity that curiosity dominated it. Neither uttered a sound for my tape, but each circled the monster warily. Horrible Harrison's lurching power is good for only about five feet, by which time his spring winds down and he groans to a halt. In each case the otter would carefully close in for a closer look as the mechanism died, and I removed the unsuccessful menace to save it for another day. I suspect that, as repulsive as the contraption was to me, to the otters it was not large enough to be taken as dangerous without further investigation. Most likely both species of otter in the wild occasionally encounter crabs that look nearly as large, and with practice learn how to dispatch them and add them to the menu. In the end I got the recordings I wanted by using the laundry bag as my Heavy.

Eventually Sam took the matter of his introduction to Mimsy into his own hands. Nobody's perfect, and on some days I am more not perfect than on others. One day, a few weeks after Sam's arrival, my footwork fell a little short. As I passed through the narrow opening of the half-width louvered door, Sam hurled himself past my feet in a slithering dash and hurtled headlong at Mimsy, giving her no choice now but to recognize his presence in the household. One way or another.

To complicate matters, Mimsy was in heat, and more than a little surly. At the moment when my guard slipped Mim had been lying supine on a towel, languorously drying herself with the slow undulation that only an otter can perform, and she was no less surprised than I at the sight of the gangling cub lolloping directly at her. Short of uttering an appropriate exclamation, which I did by the reflex of frequent practice, there was nothing at all I could do but let happen what would.

My mind flashed, not so irrelevantly, to the Christmas card I had only a week before sent to the printer. It was my custom in the past few years for the card to have an otter motif, in this case a fanciful scene that portrayed Sam and Mimsy relaxing in front of a toppled and partially demolished Christmas tree. It bore the legend "God rest ye merry, gentlemen; let nothing you dismay."

Meanwhile, back at the Moment of Truth, by the time Sam

plowed into the place where Mim had been lying she was no longer quite there. She had righted herself and in the same flowing movement side-stepped just enough to gain the advantage she needed. For a moment the two stood in frozen tableau. Mimsy's neck was arched in the reptilian fashion that I had learned to call the "punitive" posture, with the tip of her muzzle pressed to the back of Sam's neck, and a bite in the offing. I waited and hoped that Sam would utter the chuckling sound that I knew would placate her, but I knew too that this sound was probably not in Sam's hereditary vocabulary, for he had never been heard to make it before. As I feared, Sam was totally silent, and neither otter moved for long seconds; then without warning a frantic chase erupted in which otters sped through the house, thudding into furniture and changing direction like ricocheting rubber balls. My memory of the details is vague because things happened so quickly, but in spite of my difficulty in telling the two animals apart at their speed from my vantage point, my impression was that Sam was doing all of the chasing. Other than the crashing sounds of collision and the thunder of flat feet on the floor the encounter was a remarkably silent one, with none of the usual chittering of an otter meeting. In point of fact Mimsy's part in it was played reluctantly, and at the first opportunity she scooted into the bedroom and up onto my special otterproof bed, where she relaxed a little, safe for the moment from her innocent tormentor.

Sam was on the floor, too excited, I think, to realize that the chair she had used to climb to the bed was the twin of a chair in the living room that he climbed on without a second thought. Mim leaned down from her thirty-inch height and Sam stood upright; a number of times the two touched noses, and not a growl was to be heard. But Mim's nose was beginning to run and this was a certain sign that she was acutely upset. Sooner or later Sam would find that he could negotiate the chair. The only course of action left to me now was to somehow get Mimsy past her pursuer and to sanctuary in the tub, which Sam probably would not enter. I opened the shower door and called out to Mim, "Swim." She oozed like quicksilver down the chair past Sam and dashed headlong into the bathroom with Sam at her flying heels, but instead of popping into the tub she ran to ground behind the toilet. Only then did she begin to chitter at him—the loud, staccato cacophony that I had heard other otters produce under more friendly conditions of meeting. Sam, silent as usual, eventually let me lead him away and Mim retreated to the safety of the tub.

In the days that followed I let the otters meet as often as I could, and their precarious socializing seemed to alternate between partial success and utter failure. On the good days Mimsy would accept Sam's pouncing with placid dignity for a while, even seem at times to initiate a bout of wrestling, but her patience inevitably wore thin after an hour at most. Then the growling and chittering would start. In the tub she was fairly safe, for when I left the doors open Sam would loll at the rim in laughable bashful-boy postures while Mim sloshed around at breakneck speed, pausing every now and then to confront him with arched neck, to sniff slowly at his muzzle from above, below, and side while he held himself absolutely still, his eyes tightly closed.

Out in the rest of the house things sometimes took an awkward turn when Mim tried to hide behind me, keeping my feet between herself and Sam. Short of standing immobile there is no way to avoid the risk of stepping on someone, so mostly I stood still. Although Sam has since shown himself to be nervous for an otter, jumping at an unexpected touch, he was throughout his time with Mim seemingly devoid of any fear of dire consequences. Such was his aplomb that during one chase, when I could tell that Mimsy was nearing the end of her rope and I tossed out a pea, Sam swerved, caught it, and then took up the chase again, dribbling the pea before him with pushes of his nose and paws. But Sam learned in time the meaning of Mimsy's warnings in her foreign tongue. Every so often I would hear an explosive squeak from Mim followed immediately by Sam's twitter of pain, and for a few minutes at least Sam's behavior would be subdued and deferential.

In the meantime, I continued to try to make a tub-otter out of Sam. My next efforts followed the pattern of the first attempt, except that after sitting in the empty tub calling in vain to him as he lolled infuriatingly just outside, I reached out, grabbed him, and dumped him into my lap. As I had expected he bolted out without a perceptible pause. I hauled him in again and he exited again, but the third time he tarried for perhaps two entire blinks of an eye. After a few more hauls he began to stay,

and even to climb in voluntarily to rummage about under my knees. A few minutes later I stood up slowly and stepped out of the tub, while Sam, oblivious, poked around the empty tub. I let a slow trickle issue from the tap, and went to telephone Mary to boast of my achievement. As I was recounting this triumph Sam raced into the room, wet from the sides down. His wet feet slapped more loudly than was usual, and on the newly waxed floor they tended to slip sideways out from under him as he tried to negotiate a turn. From that day on, and forever more, Samaki was a full-fledged otter, and his love affair with water has been the focus of his activities. He could now join Mim in the tub where, it transpired, her attitude was a bit more tolerant than on land. Their periods together were still limited by Mimsy's temper, but it seemed to be mellowing in the long run, if not steadily or irreversibly, on a day-to-day basis. There were still tense moments when Sam would corner her and provoke a strong defense in the form of that portentous arching of the neck and the unhurried menace of her perusal of his face; Mimsy's punishing bites were always directed at Sam's face. Sam would respond in these situations with the nearly universal carnivore gesture of submissiveness, stretching out his neck and head on the floor, exposing himself to the bite if it must come, and holding himself immobile. As Konrad Lorenz has said of wolves, in the face of this sort of submissiveness the bite almost never comes, and as far as Mimsy was concerned the gesture inevitably prevented her from making good on her threat.

A few bites came my way, however, mainly during the continuation of Mimsy's nightly upset. Her nighttime behavior grew steadily worse, but I still couldn't bring myself to banish her permanently from the bedroom. For one thing, during the periods of sexual quiescence she was almost pathetically hungry for my nearness, and even though I knew that I would probably have to vacate the bed later that night, there was something about the way she would slither down alongside my calf and fall asleep in contact with me. I was reminded of the stories about werewolves who were perfectly decent by day and unaware of their nocturnal misdeeds, but it didn't help much.

I also received some bites from Sam in a more deliberate though unpremeditated way. As I've already said, Sam regarded me as more or less an equal, taking upon himself the same prerogatives I had. Thus, if Sam transgressed the bounds of what I considered to be acceptable behavior, I took measures to chastise him; Samaki, for his part did the same and, like me, he seemed at times to be able to distinguish between things I did in play and things done in anger. The quick bites he gave as Mary or I tried to keep him in his crate I've already mentioned. In these cases I believe he knew that our actions were deliberate, but if I hurt him physically in play, or whacked him when in play he bit too painfully, he never retaliated. On the other hand, once when I was on the telephone and saw him begin to lacerate the sofa cushion, I stepped over and delivered an exasperated clout. He ducked under the sofa, but I couldn't let it go at that. I had just had the cushions re-covered and for some other reason that now escapes me was not in the best of tempers, so I grabbed the disappearing tail, whereupon he whipped around and bestowed upon my forearm a restrained but angry bite. The seam of the shirt cuff took the brunt of the attack, but three canines left their marks in my flesh. Then the otter made a pass at my foot, but the bite was so softened that he left no mark. I chased him off, terminated my phone conversation, and made peace with him, a gesture that he accepted effusively.

Just as I was beginning to realize that Sam would have to be handled more subtly than my other otters, Sam too seemed to be evolving a new approach toward disciplining me. The turning point came one night when, as usual, Sam was being difficult about going into his half of the house for the night. I had found in the past few days that if I struck the floor with a short length of scrap lamp cord he would dash through the door and stay away long enough for me to get the doors shut and bolted. Sometimes this tactic failed, and when it did one light sting across the tail would do the trick. It didn't hurt him, for he never uttered any cry of pain—rather it had the psychological effect that a whack with a rolled-up newspaper has on a dog. This time, though, Sam decided that I had gone too far, and after I delivered the sting he bit my foot, quickly, silently, and efficiently. He bit forcefully enough for me to feel it but with only a fraction of the power in his jaws, power that could have driven the canines through leather, flesh, and bone. A few days later I succeeded only in getting him to the doorway, so I tried to urge him on by squeezing the door on him, slowly. Instead of scooting through he doubled back, approached my foot, and bit again. I decided then that force would no longer work and determined to use my voice instead. From a tone of cold menace I built up gradually, as my patience wore thin, to a shout. In the end I was hoarse, and Sam moved through the door at a time of his own choosing.

In retrospect it seems obvious that I should have understood his message, but Sam had to spell it out for me in terms that even a human could understand. His actions in the matter seemed to me explicable only as the result of a primitive but true reasoning process, because, like Mimsy before him, he already knew that he could get away with an out-and-out bite, and had no reason to abandon the proven method. He was in the bathroom, and for reasons best known to himself did not want to leave. I commanded him to do so in as overbearing a tone as I could muster. This time, instead of the quick bite, he gave me a symbolic one, taking my foot in his mouth and squeezing slowly down just hard enough for me to feel it. I was taken off guard. Sam looked up at me, maintaining his hold. Well, no mere otter was going to use psychology on me; this time I would make the terms of our relationship clear in no uncertain terms, so I raised my voice to its booming best. And Sam squeezed a little harder.

From that day on we have understood each other, I think, and I've adopted the strategy of seeing to it that problems are averted before they start. Mostly it works.

14 Rearrangements

If Sam had ever shown any disposition to fight back at Mimsy's hostile overtures things would never have improved, and I would have been faced with a truly impossible situation. But Sam, for all his shyness with humans and his insistence on accepting me as an equal only, is as good-natured as an animal can be, and he never once struck back at Mimsy. I have often wondered why it should be that he gave to the otter an extended respect he would not give me, particularly in view of the fact that she was, in the beginning at least, invariably hostile to him, while I was, except for isolated incidents, friendly. The explanation, I think, may lie in the obvious fact that Mimsy was another otter and I was not. By this I mean that Mimsy, at that time just barely larger than he, had the size and shape of an otter, and perhaps the cub had a built-in readiness to respond to this, while he may have had to make a greater adjustment to accept me as a companion because of my giant size and vertical alignment. Further, whatever means I used to discipline him, Mimsy had the ultimate and most natural means —her teeth. And she always applied them to the biologically proper part of him, his face, while my slowness and my ignorance often landed a slap elsewhere.

Whatever the reason, Samaki never bit back at Mimsy; goodness triumphed after a fashion, and there were times when she actually seemed to seek out his company in a playful mood. At times she accepted his pounces and returned them without the sharp squeaks and darting head movements that meant annoyance. At times she would initiate a chase or, being chased, would run with the peculiar rocking motion and slight sideways shakes of her head that expressed her good temper. But always the day of reckoning would arrive, or the hour, that turned rebuke on the cub's camaraderie.

Spring brought a new problem. Mim's behavior had more or less stabilized for the better toward Sam, and toward me for the worse, at least at night. But she began to show signs that something was wrong. Often an animal in pain turns savage, but Mim's temper remained what it was, so that it took a day or so before I could be sure that my vague feelings were justified. In retrospect, the beginning may have been on 24 February, when Mimsy had again played the virago with Sam.

She had been in the tub much of the day and now, after she had given Sam a worse time than she had in many weeks, I let her out to eat. She dried herself only partially on the towel, so after her meal I called her to the towel again and following the old custom rolled her up in it, ready to provide a brisk rubdown. Instead of squirming with delight she bit savagely through the cloth with a snarling sound, then wriggled free and came at me still snarling, a strange glassy look in her eye. I had learned long ago to proffer my foot when she was pettish, for a few restrained nips at the toe of my shoe usually satisfied her. This time she lunged repeatedly at my toe, biting so savagely that only by tipping my foot upward and presenting the sole rather than the entire tip did I avoid serious harm. For once my slovenly habits were useful; my suitcase, standing in the room since heaven knows what trip, was within reach. I snatched it up

and interposed it between us, backed out of the room and closed the door, while the demented otter continued to press the attack. Five minutes later I opened the door cautiously, only to have to close it again in the face of another onslaught.

Sam was still in the tub. I waited half an hour before trying Mim again, and used the time to figure what I would do to get him past her if she showed no improvement. My plan was elaborate and fortunately the need to implement it never arose. When I opened the door Mimsy was edgy, but seemed to have

o

come to her senses. I walked slowly into the bathroom, then released Sam from the tub. Sam dashed recklessly at her and almost miraculously she relaxed her tense posture and played with him. Not long after, they were both back in the tub as if nothing had ever happened.

Less than a week later, when I let Mim out of the tub after her night's confinement I noticed a small blood smear, and chalked it up to her estrous period. Two days later there was still blood in evidence and I began to look for another explanation. By day she used her litter pan, where the wood shavings soaked up her urine and thwarted my efforts to see if blood was present, so it became necessary to keep her under close surveillance. When I did I saw that she was in obvious pain when she urinated, and before it soaked into the shavings the urine had a pinkish tinge. Otherwise she was as active as ever and more than usually affable toward Sam.

Dr. Wolf diagnosed the disease as cystitis, an inflammation of the bladder, and gave me a sulfa drug and ammonium chloride, the latter to raise the acidity of the urine, which a test had shown to be abnormally alkaline.

Dr. Wolf had come through again. Mimsy's condition improved daily and in two weeks she was completely normal again, with the only aftereffect a possible irregularization of her next heat period.

Spring arrived in earnest and passed to summer, then fall. Life with the two otters went on very much in the established pattern, with a dash of destruction here, a minor uproar there, and about as much peaceful coexistence between the otters as Mim would allow. I wanted to attend the zoo association meetings in Milwaukee in September so, remembering how trap-shy Sam was, I brought home two large wire box traps, a week early to allow for the inevitable miscarriages of plan. Otter perversity being what it is, it was predictable that Sam would all but waltz into the trap and close the door after himself, and that Mimsy should be the difficult one. That isn't quite how it happened. Both otters were uncooperative, but Sam *was* the first to be caught, and if he didn't literally close the door behind him he did have to open it to get in. What I had done was to set the trap with its door propped open in the living room. Inside I left a trail of food, and had given Sam a light evening meal. During the night he got the food and in addition contrived to knock away the prop, so that the next morning I found myself trying to think of a better way to prop up the door. As I stood contemplating the trap Sam walked up to it, shoved his nose under the door, raised it, and sauntered in. Just as casually he exited, and since I had to quit the house for work I left the trap as it was. But I felt the taste of success as I drove to the Zoo.

I took the following day off, and in the early afternoon picked up a magazine, sat next to the trap, and waited. Not long afterward Sam was in the trap. With a single movement I jammed my foot down on the door and with a minimum of fumbling whisked a spool of wire from my pocket. I wired the door shut, then fed the otter some of his meat, in which I had mixed a tranquillizer. By the time we reached the Zoo Sam was placid almost to the point of lethargy. When I placed his trap inside one of the two large adjoining cages (built as maternity cages for tigers) he followed his old pattern of staying put. The other cage had just been outfitted with a 250-gallon stock-watering trough, so, to be sure he was all right and that he knew about the tank, I lowered his trap into the water. This did the trick, and Sam slid lazily out of the trap, hauled out of the tank, and hid behind it. I stayed long enough to satisfy myself that he was in no difficulty; then it was back home to see what could be done about Mimsy.

For some reason Mim would have nothing to do with the trap cage, and she began to avoid her old traveling case, even though it had never been removed from the room in all the months past. She had often slept in it. It was as familiar to her as any of the house's furnishings. I tried the customary act of spreading a towel in it and, when that failed to attract her, removed all the other towels from sight. I put food into it. I placed it in the empty tub with her, but by now her suspicions were aroused if they hadn't been before. At last I attempted to lower it over her, only to be rewarded by two bites on the ankle, followed by a renewed attack. These were "punishing" bites, though, made with the mouth only partly open so that only her small incisors made contact with me—not the real bites of her madness when with fully open mouth she attempted to drive her long canines into me. I beat a hasty retreat. Next day I managed to get her into the travel case and reunited her with Sam at the Zoo. Between them they saw to it that the big tank was not neglected, and other than a little chirping from Mim when I left the nursery room they seemed not to mind my departure, or their new quarters.

For a variety of reasons, when I returned from Mikwaukee at the end of the month I let the otters stay at the Zoo for five weeks before finally making what had become a terribly difficult choice—that Mimsy would remain at the Zoo. I listed and relisted my reasons mentally. She had become totally unmanageable for much of the time—potentially dangerous, in fact; she had never really accepted Sam but for a few days on and off; she seemed perfectly content at the Zoo, where she could swim whenever she wanted to. Lastly there was Harry, a recently widowed North American otter with a gentle tolerant disposition, with whom I had long hoped to mate her. On the side of bringing her home again I had only one argument, that she had once been a trustworthy animal and that no matter how hellish she could now be she was a part of my life. Had it not been for Harry I most likely would have let the last argument outweigh the others, but in the end Mimsy stayed.

With the arrival of warm weather, she was introduced to Harry in his outdoor enclosure. Mimsy treated him as abominably as she had Sam, despite Harry's gentlemanly restraint and much greater size. She seemed to be trying to make his life one of unalloyed misery, but if she succeeded Harry never gave any sign; he seemed happy to have her company. Summer passed, taking Mim into heat and out at her old pace, while Harry, whose species comes into heat briefly in the cold part of the year only, put up with her more shrewish interludes. In the last week of October Harry's fancy at last turned to thoughts of love—by no means lightly—and at the same time Mim came into another estrous period.

Emil Liers, my boyhood idol and now my friend, was the first man to breed North American otters, and has kept hundreds over the past thirty or forty years. He had told me how much individual otters of the same species differ in temperament, and how impossible it is to get just any pair of otters to breed unless they meet one another's standards for compatibility. Some males, he said, are too rough for a given female, while others aren't rough enough to overcome the average female's ugly temper when in heat. Harry, henpecked all summer and most of the fall, turned out to be an ideal mate. While the reproductive urge stirred him he asserted himself just enough to subdue his seemingly reluctant mate, but not a bite more. For a week the otters gave the impression that they were devoting their full waking hours, with brief time out for feeding, to the business of sex. Mimsy would repulse every insult to her maidenhood (or after the first time, to its memory) with loud protests and bites. Harry took her abuse and persevered, until he could grasp the nape of her neck tightly in his teeth. Then they would roll over and over in the water, and none of the observers over that week ever reported anything but rape. Or so it seemed; the truth is that the protests are all a part of the game where otters are concerned.

We never saw whether Harry's advances were physically successful because the activity took place in the water, which was always churned up by the violence of the honeymoon. But Mimsy missed her next two heat periods, so it was a safe bet that she was pregnant.

The next question on the agenda was when we could expect the birth, if it would take place at all. To begin with, the two otters, Peruvian Mim and North American Harry, supposedly belonged to different species, although there are some of us who believe them to be only members of different races of a single species. Whichever the case, the North American otter has but one breeding season a year, and the fertilized egg, after undergoing a few cell divisions, becomes dormant while it still floats free in the uterus. The breeding season takes place in late winter and not until the following January or February does the blastocyst, as the divided egg is called, implant in the uterine wall and begin to develop in earnest. No one knows what takes place in South American otters. The phenomenon of delayed implantation is apparently a device to insure the first ventures by cubs from the nest when warm weather arrives; in the tropics no such need should exist, and probably for that reason breeding is not limited by season, nor should delayed implantation be necessary.

So what about Mimsy? Toward the end of December, when

nearly two months had passed, we brought her indoors—separating her from Harry would have been necessary in any event, since mother otters in captivity as well as in the wild drive their mates away and keep them away for the first few months of their cubs' lives. Inside, Mim settled down nicely, and her teats showed some signs of enlargement, I thought. But the sixty-one days passed, then ninety days, and no cubs appeared. About that time workmen arrived to make necessary repairs in the building, and the noise seemed to upset the otter. A few days later a keeper saw some blood in Mim's enclosure. Probably she aborted the cubs and ate the remains—whether because of the disturbance or because of some physiological incompatibility in the chemistry of the developing cubs, we don't know. Perhaps the two kinds of otter *are* too dissimilar to produce viable offspring. I doubt that such is the case, and keep the hope that next year things will turn out better. Mimsy and Harry have been reunited again, and she treats him no more considerately. Harry, as usual, doesn't mind and, as Sam did, seems to put up with her for the sake of her good days.

Now to return to the previous November: I was ready to bring Sam home, and I had some misgivings because in the Zoo he had became as shy of me as of anyone who visited him. He entered the trap without his usual procrastination, and we set off for home. In the car he sought no reassurance from me and we might have been complete strangers. But in the house, no sooner had he stepped from the trap than he shuffled over to me to poke his nose familiarly against my ankle, and a minute later we were hand-wrestling on the floor as if he had never been away. Later he paused, and without a trace of hesitation proceeded to his old litter pan to put it to its old use. Then he came back for another tussle. By the end of the following day the floors were wet and slippery enough again to make me walk

with short careful steps. Small bits and frazzles of what had been toys once more lay scattered underfoot and the house was taking on the look and the scent of an otter's den once more.

It would be a good thing, I suppose, if I could end now with an incident in keeping with the otter panache. But Sam has let me down. By the time of his nonchalant homecoming he had grown a shade more mature, and for an otter almost staid. The

resumption of our lives together, our dual bachelorhood, pro-
gressed in quiet routine for quite a long time, and this era of
tranquillity is a fitting place to end.

Of course my concept of quiet routine isn't quite what it used
to be.